A Comprehensive Guide to

SIGN LANGUAGE INTERPRETING

IN EUROPE

2012 edition

Maya de Wit

ISBN 978-90-806571-4-4

Author: Maya de Wit

Front cover: Vivian van Schagen

Publisher: M. de Wit

CONTENTS

FOREWORD

My first real encounter with sign language occurred at the Maryland School for the Blind in Baltimore in 1989. I lived at the school during my year-long internship for my BA in recreation. At the school there were Deafblind children who had few adults they could communicate with through tactile sign language. From that moment on I became fascinated with sign language and I learned American Sign Language through books and meeting Deaf and hearing sign language users.

Since then I have become an RID registered American Sign Language interpreter and completed my BA as Dutch Sign Language interpreter. I was also privileged to participate in the first group of students of the European Master in Sign Language Interpreting (EUMASLI). With 16 sign language interpreters from across Europe we studied together for 2.5 years and finally presented our MA theses at a specially organized seminar in Italy in September 2011. My MA research explored the view of Deaf persons on their quality of life while being enrolled in inclusive education with a sign language interpreter. One of the outcomes was a set of indicators within specific domains which have an effect on the quality of life of Deaf persons in education with an interpreter.

From 2006 till 2012 I had the honor to be the president of the European Forum of Sign Language Interpreters (efsli). Working together with interpreters and Deaf people at a European level was an inspiring, rewarding and enjoyable learning environment. I learned many new skills in sign language, communication, funding applications and reports and gained knowledge of different cultures, (sign) languages, and the world of the European Union. It was the best schooling I have ever had. Besides the knowledge and skills, I met many old and new colleagues, friends and stakeholders across all borders. The people, their involvement and their aspirations, were my inspiration and motivation.

I am unable to thank everyone individually, but this new edition of the publication 'Sign Language Interpreting in Europe' is my thank you to all of you and especially to all my efsli friends. Without your support and enthusiasm I would not be where I am today.

I would also like to thank all the respondents who filled out the survey and answered additional questions following the survey. Without your help this publication would never have been realized. And thank you to the many people who encouraged me to continue my search for data and to publish an update on sign language interpreting in Europe.

Maya de Wit, September 2012

LIST OF RESPONDENTS

Albania	Kosovo
Austria	Latvia
Belgium - Flanders	Lithuania
Belgium - Wallonia	Malta
Bosnia and Herzegovina	Netherlands
Croatia	Norway
Cyprus	Poland
Czech Republic	Portugal
Denmark	Romania
England, Wales & Northern Ireland	Russia
Estonia	Scotland
Finland	Serbia - ATSZJ
France	Serbia - UTLOSS
Germany	Slovenia
Greece	Spain
Hungary	Sweden
Iceland	Switzerland - French region
Ireland	Switzerland - German region
Italy - ANIMU	Switzerland - Italian region
Italy - ANIOS	Ukraine

INTRODUCTION

The profession of sign language interpreting is developing rapidly across Europe. Since the publication of the first edition of Sign language interpreting in Europe in 2000, the profession has undergone many changes, such as an increase in the educational and training opportunities for interpreters and the establishment of national associations of sign language interpreters.

This fourth edition of *Sign Language Interpreting in Europe* provides an overview of the current situation of the sign language interpreting profession in 2012. The data published in this publication is based on a European wide survey. A total of 40 countries and regions responded to the survey, which was sent out in the spring of 2012. The countries and regions are within the region of the Council of Europe, which currently consists of 47 countries.[1]

In 2000 in the first survey, nineteen countries participated. The data from the first survey and the data in the surveys in 2004, 2007, and now in 2012, show which trends shaped the sign language interpreter profession during the last dozen years. The survey consists of questions concerning organizations that represent the interests of interpreters in areas such as education, employment, remuneration, and legislation. The survey was sent to all national associations of sign language interpreters in the countries. In countries which do not have an association for sign language interpreters, the survey was answered by national Deaf association. The list of all the respondents is on page 8.

The responses reveal diversity in the sign language interpreter profession between the countries and regions. The status of the profession in the countries is strongly related to the national existing laws and regulations (Wheatley & Pabsch, 2012). In addition, there is noticeable influence of the national history and culture of the individual countries on the profession (de Wit & Wheatley, forthcoming). Throughout the last decade, the developments in the profession can be identified by different phases: establishment of education and training for interpreters, provision of interpreting services, founding of national associations of interpreters, design of regulations and rights of Deaf sign language users to interpreting services, and the latest development: the establishment of national registration bodies for professional sign language interpreters (de Wit, 2001; 2004; 2008).

This publication consists of three main parts on organizations, education and employment. The appendices provide the additional results from the survey which are not discussed in detail in the three chapters. In addition, appendix 6 provides 'Facts and figures per country'. At the end, following part 3, a short conclusion is provided.

---

1. http://www.coe.int/aboutcoe/index.asp?page=47pays1europe (Last accessed 10 September 2012)

PART 1 – ORGANIZATIONS

1.1 ESTABLISHMENT OF SIGN LANGUAGE INTERPRETER ORGANIZATIONS

National sign language interpreter associations in Europe are present within a country or a language region. The majority of the respondents indicate that they have a national organization for sign language interpreters in their country or organization. For an overview of all the organizations, please refer to appendix 6 'Facts and figures per country'.

The first national organization of sign language interpreters was established in Sweden in 1969. Three Scandinavian countries were the first countries to set up an organization of interpreters. After Sweden, Denmark and Norway followed in 1977. In 1978 France was the first non-Scandinavian country to set up an organization. The youngest organizations are the newly established associations in 2011 in Ireland (CISLI), and in Portugal (ANAPILG). Ireland and Portugal previously had associations which had folded. Since the last survey in 2007, new associations have been established in Belgium-Flanders, Ireland, Kosovo, Lithuania, Poland, Portugal, Romania, Russia and Serbia-ATSZJ.

Not all countries participating in the survey provided the year of establishment. Figure 1.1 lists the organizations that are officially independent interpreter organizations and which gave a year of establishment.

Country	Name	Year established	Country	Name	Year established
Sweden	STTF	1969	Germany	BGSD	1997
Norway	Tolkeforbundet	1977	Austria	ÖGSDV	1998
Denmark	FTT	1977	Iceland	HART	1999
France	AFILS	1978	Spain	FILSE	2000
Scotland	SASLI	1981	Czech Republic	CKTZJ	2000
Finland	SVT	1982	Serbia	UTLOSS	2000
England, Wales & NI	ASLI	1986	Switzerl. – It.	ILISSI	2001
Belgium - Wallonia	ABILS	1986	Belgium	VVTG	2001 - 2009
Ireland	IASLI	1987 - 2007	Slovenia	ZTZJ	2004
Italy (ANIMU)	ANIMU	1987	Kosovo	KASLI	2008
Italy (ANIOS)	ANIOS	1987	Romania	ANIALMG	2008
Netherlands	NBTG	1988	Belgium	BVGT	2009
Estonia	EVTKŰ	1989	Lithuania	GKVA	2009
Greece	SDENG	1991	Poland	STPJM	2009
Portugal		1991 - ?	Serbia	ATSZJ	2010
Switzerl. – Ge. region	bgd	1991	Russia	RASLI	2010
Switzerl. – Fr. region	ARILS	1992	Ireland	CISLI	2011
Hungary	JOSZ	1994	Portugal	ANAPILG	2011

Fig. 1.1: Year of establishment of independent interpreter organizations

1.2   NATIONAL ORGANIZATIONS

Some countries have more than one national association, such as Serbia, Italy, Belgium, Switzerland, and the United Kingdom. Switzerland officially has four spoken languages: German, French, Italian, and Rhaeto-Romance. The three associations for sign language interpreters (ARILS, BGD & ILISSI) in Switzerland are linked to the regions of Switzerland where German Sign Language (BGD), French Sign Language (ARILS), and Italian Sign Language (ILISSI) are used.

Belgium is, like Switzerland, a country with more than one official spoken language, namely French, Flemish, and German. Since there is such a linguistic difference between the north and the south, anything pertaining to sign language interpreting is taken care of separately (M. van Herreweghe & M. van Nuffel, 2000).2 The sign language interpreters in the Flemish part of Belgium have an organization the BVGT. There is an organization for interpreters in Wallonia, the French speaking part, which is called ABILS.

In Serbia, UTLOSS was established in 2000 and ATZSJ in 2010. The organizations state to have specific and differing visions on how to move forward their profession (efsli Newsletter, March 2011). Both organizations became a full member of the European Forum of Sign Language Interpreters (efsli) in 2011.

In Italy the two associations for sign language interpreters (ANIOS & ANIMU) have a different history.

> *"For many years you could become a Sign Language Interpreter in Italy after the attendance of two years of Sign language classes at various levels, different amount of hours, etc. The Deaf Association (ENS) held every number of years a National Standardization Exam. Anyone with any kind of sign language certification could take the exam and after passing the exam you were registered in the National Register of ENS. At the same time Regional vocational courses started and provided a Vocational Qualification as Communicators, and/or Sign Language Interpreters. One of these courses was set up by the Regional Council of "Marche", all the qualified students from that Region organized an association at that level. The Deaf Association holding only a Register thought that was appropriate to organize the members of the Register in an Association. So some of the members of the Register became part of ANIMU (National Association of the Interpreters for the Hearing Impaired). The Regional Association of "Marche" with other members of the register became an independent (from ENS) national association of interpreters by the name of ANIOS (originally "National Association of Interpreters and Operators for the Deaf", and now "Association of Italian Sign Language Interpreters"). Both Interpreters' Associations are at national level. The reason to have two associations was to work independently, especially on the financial side, from the customers (Deaf People) represented by the Deaf Association (ENS). Since then, ANIMU, has gained control of their finances and are now an independent association, and even though there is no "raison d'etre" for two associations, the philosophies are often very different."3*

Most national organizations for sign language interpreters in Europe are directly linked to a single sign language rather than to one European country. If a country has more than one spoken language, it has at least an equivalent number of sign languages. The exceptions are Scotland and

---

2 RID Journal of Interpretation 2000: Sign (Language) Interpreting in Flanders, Belgium

3 June 2001, Interview by e-mail with an Italian Sign Language interpreter, member of ANIOS

England, Wales & Northern Ireland. The latter all use British Sign Language, yet Scotland has their own distinct organization. Therefore, in this publication when referring to the United Kingdom a distinction is made between Scotland and England, Wales & Northern Ireland.

The countries with more than one association provide several reasons for not having one national association per country such as language, culture, geography, and regional rules and regulations. If interpreters do not share the same (spoken) language, communicating and working together in one organization is challenging or even impossible.

1.3   NAMES OF THE ORGANIZATIONS

Most of the independent organizations of sign language interpreters are called organization or association of sign language interpreters and have added their nationality to it. There are a few exceptions to this. The national organization in Norway which was first called the NFDD (Norwegian Association of Interpreters for the Deaf and Deafblind has changed their name to Tolkeforbundet (Association of interpreters). In 2001 their name already differed from other associations, explicitly called "(...) Interpreters for the Deaf and Deafblind". All the other association had their national sign language in the name of the association.

FILSE, the Spanish association, has in the past added "Guide-Interpreters" to their name: "Spanish Federation of Spanish Sign Language Interpreters and Guide-Interpreters."

1.4   COUNTRIES WITHOUT AN INDEPENDENT NATIONAL INTERPRETER ORGANIZATION

The countries which do not have an independent national association of sign language interpreters are Albania, Bosnia, Croatia, Cyprus, Latvia, Malta and Ukraine. Some of these countries, such as Latvia and the Ukraine have a sub-organization or committee for interpreters within or under the national Deaf organization. Turkey did not respond to this questionnaire but an interpreter organization was established in the spring of 2011 (efsli, personal email correspondence, May 2011). Croatia also established an association in 2009 (HDPZJ), which unfortunately folded in 2011. The working conditions for sign language interpreters in Croatia did not improve, and interpreters were forced to find other forms of employment, which resulted in termination of the association's work. Hungary formally has a national association of sign language interpreters, but the association has been inactive for some years. SINOSZ, the Hungarian Deaf Association, filled out the survey in relation to the current status of sign language interpreters in Hungary.

1.5   PERCENTAGE OF MEMBERS

One of the questions in the survey concerns the number of sign language interpreters in the country or region which are a member of their national association. Not all respondents were able to answer this question, because of the unavailability of data (Belgium-Wallonia, Croatia-DODIR, Denmark, England/Wales/NI, Germany, Hungary, Serbia-UTLOSS and Sweden).

In the last survey in 2007, the regions in Switzerland had the highest percentage; most of the interpreters were a member of their affiliated organization. ARILS the Swiss organization in the French part of Switzerland and the organization in the German part (bgd), both nearly count 100% of all interpreters as a member of their organizations. In the Italian speaking part (ILISSI) of Switzerland it is estimated that eighty percent is a member.

Spain, Serbia-ATSZJ, Poland, and Portugal indicate to have the lowest relative membership, under 20%. Spain has the largest number of interpreters in Europe, but only 10% is a member of FILSE. Figure 1.2 indicates the percentage of interpreter members per country. The countries that do not have an organization of sign language interpreters or did not have the data are not mentioned in the figure.

Fig. 1.2: Sign Language Interpreters and national organizations: relative membership

■ members
■ not members

Country	members
Spain	10
Δ Russia	13
Δ Serbia-ATSZJ	20
Δ Poland	20
Δ Portugal	20
Norway	25
France	30
Δ Belgium-...	40
Slovenia	44
Italy - ANIOS	50
Italy - ANIMU	50
Czech Republic	60
Iceland	70
Δ Ireland	70
Estonia	76
Switzerl.-ILISSI	80
Austria	80
Finland	83
Netherlands	87
Δ Kosovo	90
Greece	95
Δ Lithuania	95
Scotland	95
Switz.-Fr.	97
Switz.-Ge.	99

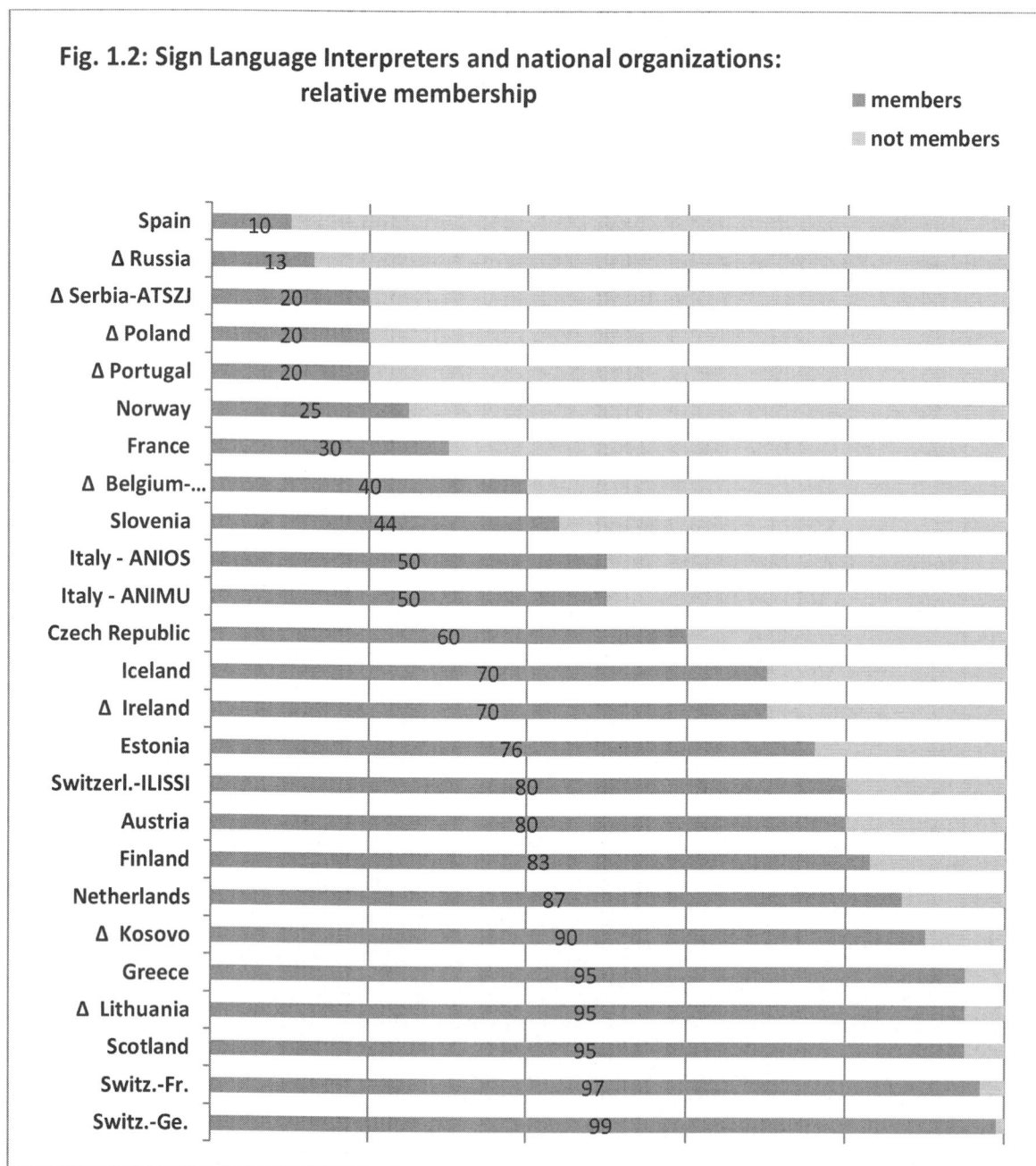

Δ New association since last survey in 2007
• Former association, now folded

1.6 MEMBERSHIP NUMBERS

SVT the national association of sign language interpreters in Finland has the highest number of interpreter members: 655 (figure 1.3). In the past surveys Spain held the leading position in the number of interpreter members, but is now in third place (500 members) after England, Wales, & Northern Ireland (639 interpreter members). The top six countries all saw an increase of their interpreter membership, with the exception of Spain which saw a decrease of nearly 6% in interpreter members. FILSE, the Spanish association of sign language interpreters notes that the reported percentage of interpreter membership is based on the total number of qualified interpreters (5000+), not the number of working SLIs, which is assumed to be much lower.

Another decrease can be seen with the Norwegian association which had 370 interpreter members in 2007 and now has 111 interpreter members left. The same trend can be seen by another Scandinavian country, namely Sweden which has 146 interpreter members, compared to the previous 279 members. Spain, Norway, Sweden, and the Italian speaking part of Switzerland are the only countries and regions that show a decrease in interpreter members, all other respondents witness an increase.

Three of the countries which have associations with large membership numbers (Finland, England, Wales & Northern Ireland, and the Netherlands) are experiencing an increase of more than 50% in their interpreter membership since 2007:

- Finland: 50%

- England, Wales & Northern Ireland: 56%

- Netherlands: 70%

With an increase of 70% the NBTG is again the fastest growing interpreter association in Europe in the last five years. The cause can be found in the number of interpreters graduating from the interpreter program and the active membership drive. From 1997 till 2001, no interpreters graduated in the Netherlands. In 2001 the first interpreters graduated from the new BA interpreting program. Two more associations saw their membership grow rapidly, the BGSD in Germany (27%) and the FTT in Denmark (33%).

The associations in the smaller countries and regions, such as the Italian speaking part of Switzerland (ILISSI) have the least number of interpreter members (10), followed by Romania (14), Estonia (23) and Iceland (25). The first larger country on the list with a relatively small number of interpreter members is Poland. SPTJM, the new association for sign language interpreters in Poland, which was established in 2009. Their first national conference was held in December 2011 (efsli Newsletter, spring 2012).

Fig. 1.3: Number of interpreters that are a member of their national or regional organization

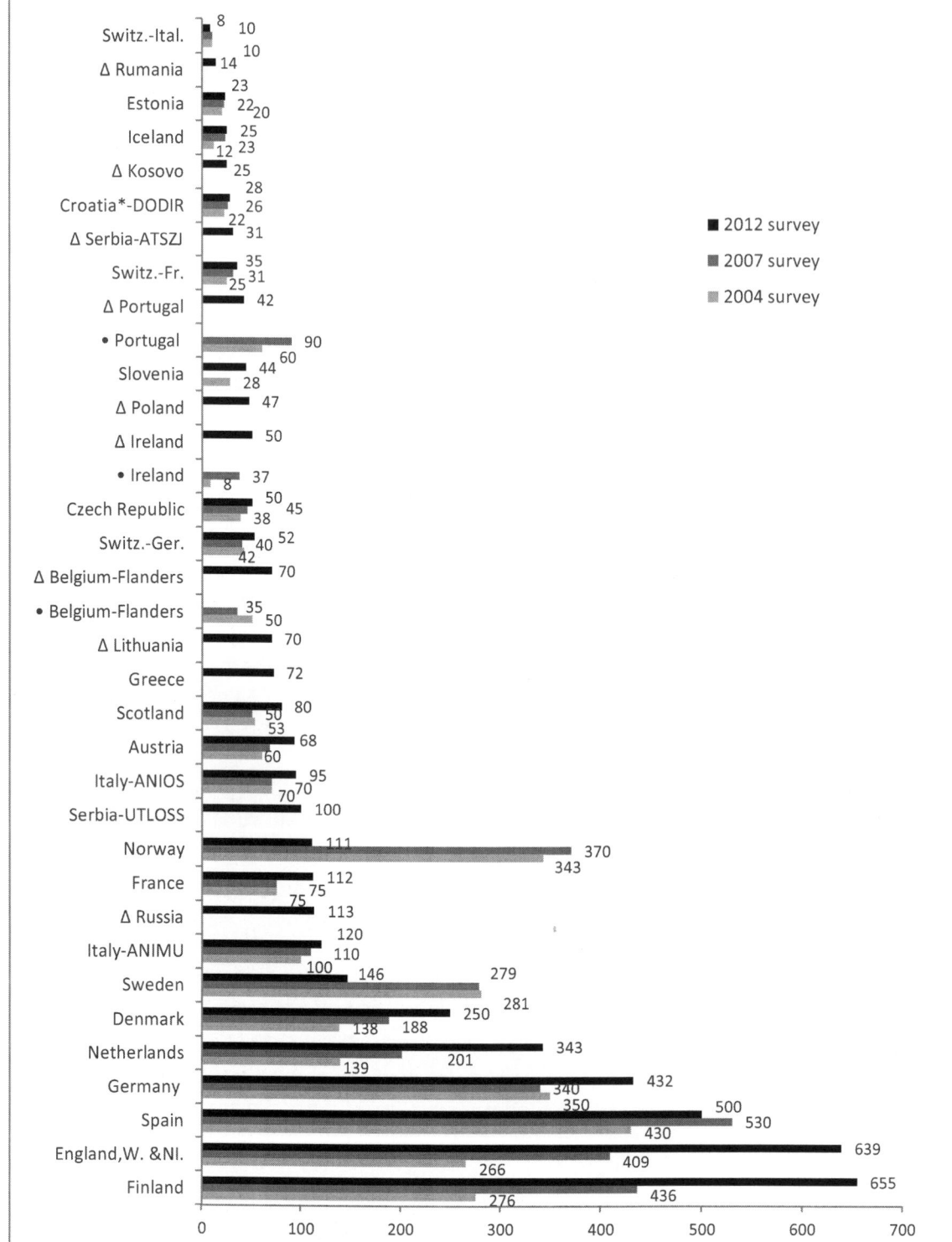

Legend:
- 2012 survey
- 2007 survey
- 2004 survey

Country	2012	2007	2004
Switz.-Ital.	8	10	
Δ Rumania	14	10	
Estonia	23	22	20
Iceland	25	23	
Δ Kosovo	12	25	
Croatia*-DODIR	28	26	
Δ Serbia-ATSZJ	22	31	
Switz.-Fr.	35	31	
Δ Portugal	25		
• Portugal	42	90	60
Slovenia	44	28	
Δ Poland	47		
Δ Ireland	50		
• Ireland	37	8	
Czech Republic	50	45	38
Switz.-Ger.	52	40	42
Δ Belgium-Flanders	70		
• Belgium-Flanders	35	50	
Δ Lithuania	70		
Greece	72		
Scotland	80	50	53
Austria	68	60	
Italy-ANIOS	95	70	70
Serbia-UTLOSS	100		
Norway	111	370	343
France	112	75	75
Δ Russia	113		
Italy-ANIMU	120	110	
Sweden	100	146	279
Denmark	281	250	138 188
Netherlands	343	201	139
Germany	432	340	350
Spain	500	530	430
England,W. &NI.	639	409	266
Finland	655	436	276

Δ New association since last survey in 2007

• Former association, now folded

* Sign Language Interpreters that are part of another organization

1.7   DEAF INTERPRETERS AS A MEMBER

Internationally the demand for Deaf sign language interpreters is growing (conclusions from the efsli Working Seminar I, November 2011). Deaf interpreters work in a variety of settings, interpreting within a team with hearing sign language interpreters, interpreting between two sign languages or systems and translating between written text and sign language. Examples of interpreting situations involve consumers with minimal language skills, legal settings, Deaf people who use a foreign sign language, interpreting for Deafblind persons (e.g. tactile), and mental health.

Only a few countries have professional interpreter training for (prospective) Deaf interpreters (see chapter 2 'Education'). As a result, few countries recognize this as a profession and membership within the professional organization of sign language interpreters is not possible. The organizations that have Deaf interpreters as a member are DODIR (Croatia), CKTZJ (Czech Republic), ASLI (England, Wales & Northern Ireland), SVT (Finland), JOSZ (Hungary), CISLI (Ireland), RASLI (Russia), and AILGP (Portugal).

1.8   NON-INTERPRETER MEMBERSHIP TO INTERPRETER ORGANIZATIONS

Some organizations also have non-interpreters as a member of their organization. Non-interpreters can be students, Deaf people, trainers, other professionals, organizations, or businesses.

The majority of the associations indicate that they also have students as members of the association. The eight associations which only have interpreter members are Austria, France, Greece, Lithuania, Portugal, Slovenia and Switzerland (ARILS & ILISSI). Next to student membership, some associations also have institutes (Czech Republic, Finland, Hungary, Serbia-UTLOSS, England/W/NI) as members and trainers (Croatia-DODIR, Finland, Germany, Italy-ANIMU, Kosovo, Poland). Italy-ANIOS indicates that they have the possibility for supportive members, but they have no members in that category at this moment.

All the organizations have more interpreter members than non-interpreter members. There are nine associations with interpreter members only. Noticeable is the high number of non-interpreter members (40) that CKTZJ (Czech Republic) has in relation to the number of interpreter members (50).

The Netherlands is the organization with the most non-interpreter members (182). The NBTG has had an active policy to recruit and inform more students, related professionals, and organizations in the field. The non-interpreter members receive information through the quarterly newsletter of the NBTG, which publishes information on the organization and on the profession of sign language interpreting. The newsletter has become an important medium in the interpreting and Deaf community.

Fig. 1.4: Number of interpreters & non-interpreter members who are a member of the national or regional organization

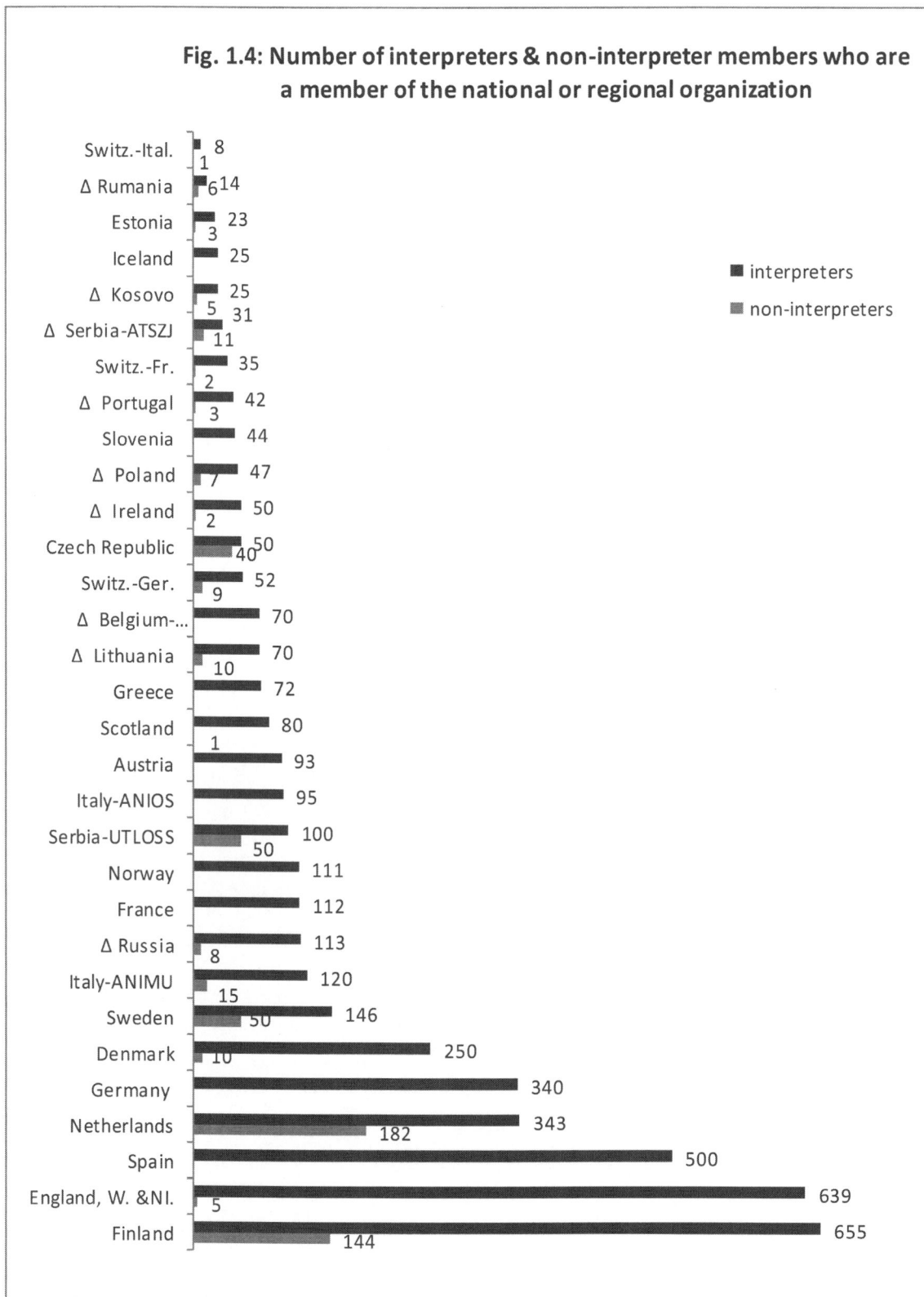

Legend:
- interpreters
- non-interpreters

Country	interpreters	non-interpreters
Switz.-Ital.	8	1
Δ Rumania	14	6
Estonia	23	3
Iceland	25	
Δ Kosovo	25	5
Δ Serbia-ATSZJ	31	11
Switz.-Fr.	35	2
Δ Portugal	42	3
Slovenia	44	
Δ Poland	47	7
Δ Ireland	50	2
Czech Republic	50	40
Switz.-Ger.	52	9
Δ Belgium-...	70	
Δ Lithuania	70	10
Greece	72	
Scotland	80	1
Austria	93	
Italy-ANIOS	95	
Serbia-UTLOSS	100	50
Norway	111	
France	112	
Δ Russia	113	8
Italy-ANIMU	120	15
Sweden	146	50
Denmark	250	10
Germany	340	
Netherlands	343	182
Spain	500	
England, W. &NI.	639	5
Finland	655	144

Δ New association since last survey in 2007

Fig. 1.5: Number of Sign Language Interpreters in 23 European countries, estimated by membership percentage of the corresponding national assocation

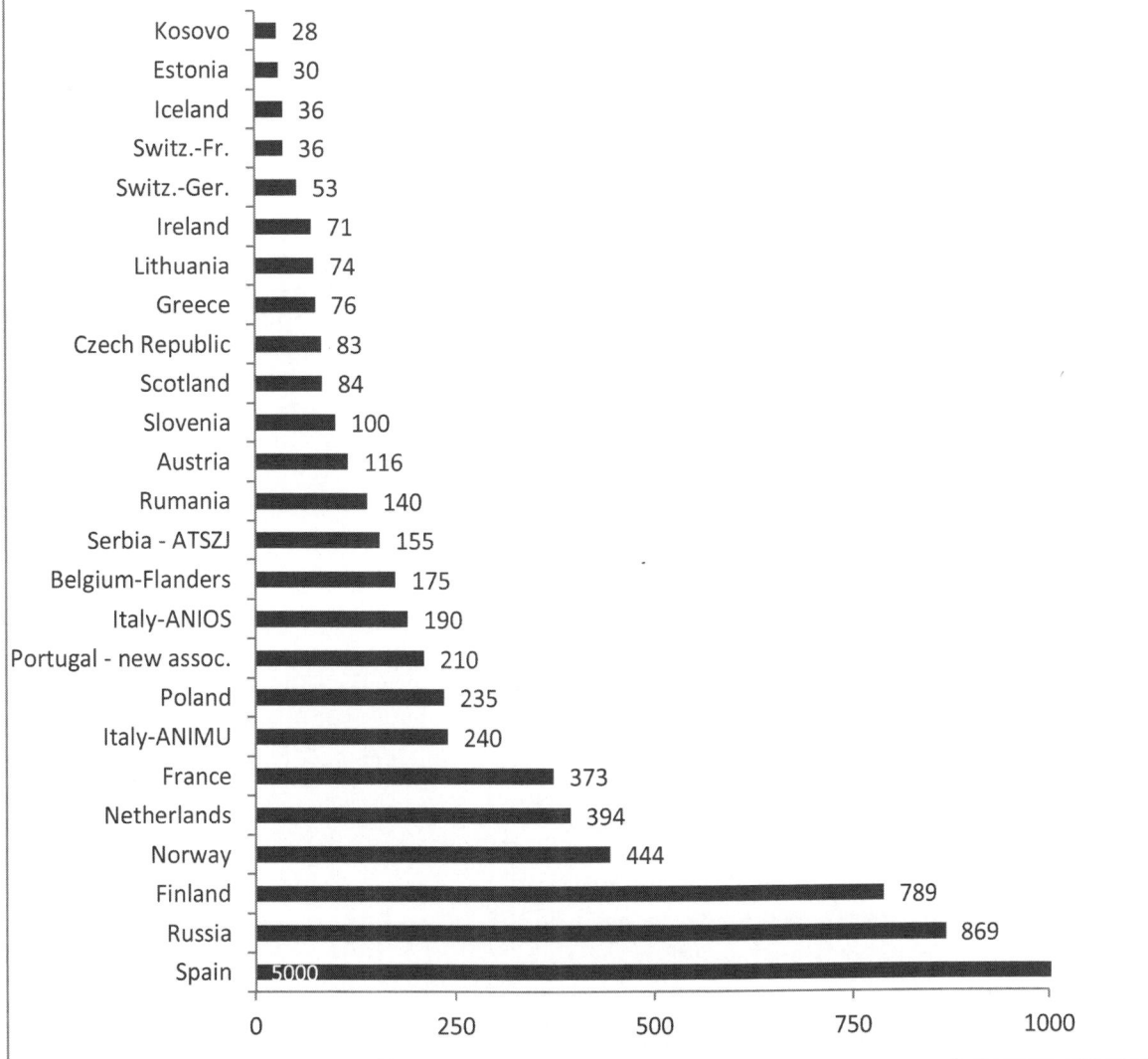

Kosovo	28
Estonia	30
Iceland	36
Switz.-Fr.	36
Switz.-Ger.	53
Ireland	71
Lithuania	74
Greece	76
Czech Republic	83
Scotland	84
Slovenia	100
Austria	116
Rumania	140
Serbia - ATSZJ	155
Belgium-Flanders	175
Italy-ANIOS	190
Portugal - new assoc.	210
Poland	235
Italy-ANIMU	240
France	373
Netherlands	394
Norway	444
Finland	789
Russia	869
Spain	5000

Not included: Countries without an association as well as Croatia-DODIR, Denmark, England/Wales/NI, Germany, Hungary, Serbia-UTLOSS, and Sweden.

1.9 NUMBER OF SIGN LANGUAGE INTERPRETERS BASED ON MEMBERSHIP PERCENTAGE

Based on the numbers given by the national and regional associations, an estimate is made on the number of sign language interpreters (fig. 1.5). The countries which do not have an association are not included in figure 1.5. In the 23 countries, there are an estimated 10,001 sign language interpreters. These numbers do not imply that all of the 10,001 are actually working as an interpreter. In part 3, 'Employment', the actual numbers are given on the interpreters who are currently working in all European countries.

Fig. 1.6: National organizations - individual interpreter membership fee (in Euros)

Country	2012	2007
Δ Serbia-ATSZJ	4,27	
Δ Lithuania	5,80	
Serbia-UTLOSS	10,00	
Estonia	10,00	6,40
Croatia*	10,00	
Δ Poland	10,00	11,50
Δ Rumania	15,00	
Iceland	18,50	11,00
Hungary	20,00	6,00
Δ Kosovo	20,00	
Czech Republic	23,20	8,00
Δ Portugal	24,00	
Δ Russia	24,00	
Δ Belgium-BVGT	34,31	20,00
Switz. - ILISSI	42,00	30,00
Sweden	42,00	38,00
Spain	50,00	50,00
France	60,00	55,00
Denmark	66,66	43,00
Italy-ANIMU	80,00	50,00
Norway	91,67	70,00
Δ Ireland	100,00	
Germany	130,00	100,00
Italy-ANIOS	130,00	130,00
Austria	150,00	100,00
Greece	150,00	
Switz.-Fr.	150,00	140,00
Netherlands	230,00	225,00
England, W & NI	252,00	271,00
Scotland	296,55	256,00
Switz.-Ger.	312,00	225,00

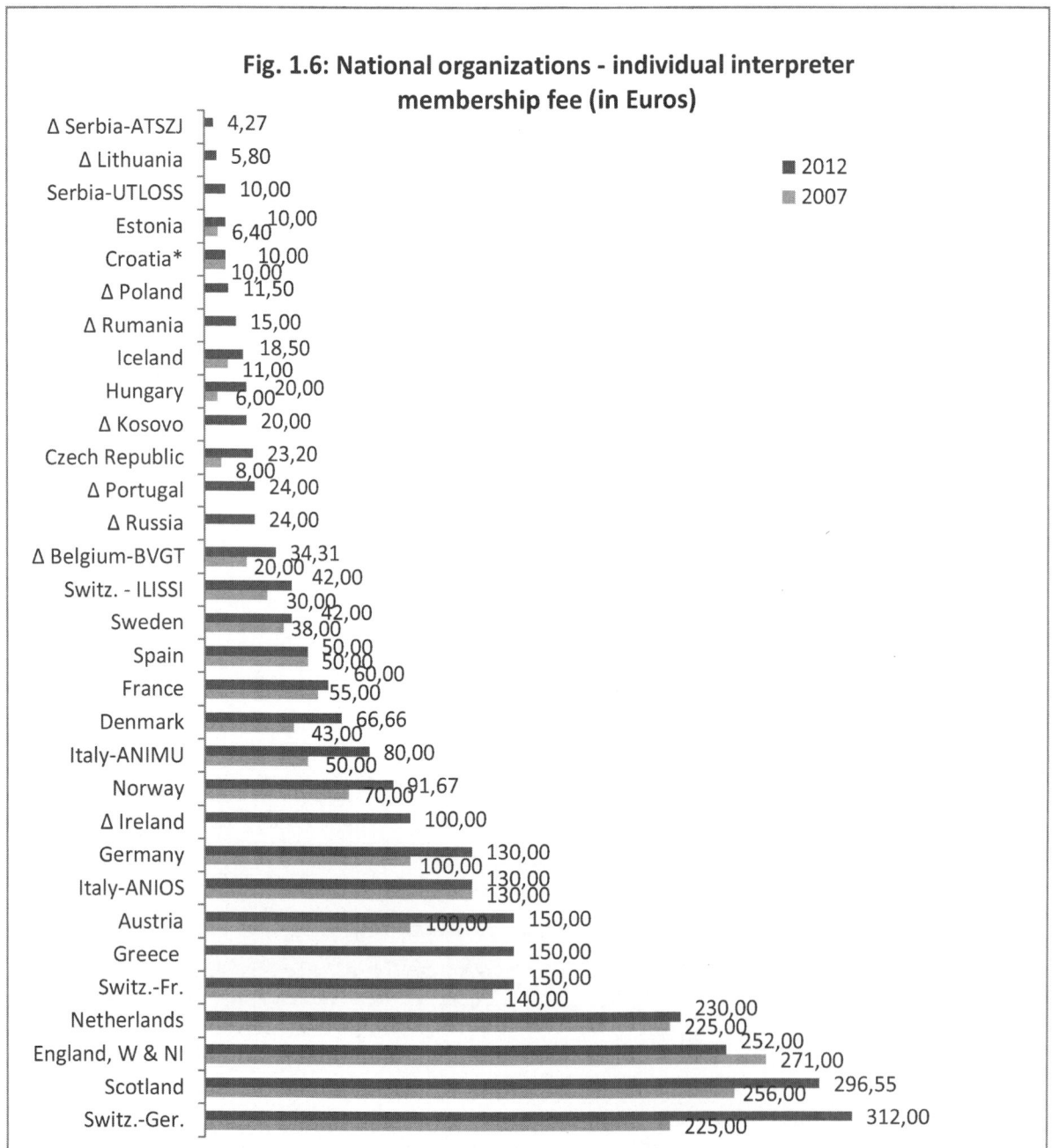

1.10 MEMBERSHIP FEES

There are vast differences between organizations membership fees (figure 1.6). One reason for this can be the economic situation of the respective countries and the income of the interpreters. The Eastern European countries report the lowest membership fees, with the exception of Belgium-Flanders (BVGT) and Iceland which have a relative low membership fee compared to the Western European countries. The BVGT, the Flemish association for sign language interpreters, notes that their annual membership fee (€ 34,31) is equal to the government rate for one interpreting hour. The German region of Switzerland has the highest membership fee (€ 312,00). This could also be due to the current exchange rate of the Swiss Franc to the Euro (September 2012). In second place is Scotland (SASLI) with nearly 300 euros per year, followed by ASLI, the association of England, Wales & Northern Ireland, which yet saw a sharp membership increase.

All the associations see an increase in their membership fee since 2007, except DODIR in Croatia, whose membership is still 10 euros per year.

In Denmark the interpreters are members of different unions (SL and HK). SL members receive a 10 euro discount on their membership paid by the union. SVT, the Finish Association of Sign Language interpreters, is the only organization that has a membership fee without a set rate for each interpreter member. The SVT has a system where the interpreter member pays a fee of 1.3% of the interpreter's gross earnings. This fee includes also the service of the unemployment fund. Student members of SVT do not pay a membership fee. The German association (BGSD) has a similar policy.

The FILSE (Spain) membership fee of 50 euros is an average. Each Spanish regional association sets its own fee. For their affiliation to FILSE, the associations pay FILSE 15 euros per member.

1.11 TOTAL MEMBERSHIP FEE PER ASSOCIATION

Based on the number of interpreter members (fig. 1.3) and the membership fee per individual member (fig. 1.6), the total amount of membership fees per association can be calculated (fig. 1.7). Figure 1.7 provides an overview of the total amount an association receives annually in individual interpreter membership fees.

Some associations have additional categories of membership. The fees for these memberships are not included in figure 1.7. Slovenia does not receive any membership fees, therefore they have no income on membership. The highest income has ASLI, the Association of Sign Language Interpreters in England, Wales, and Northern Ireland.

Fig. 1.7: Total individual membership fees per year per national association (in Euros)

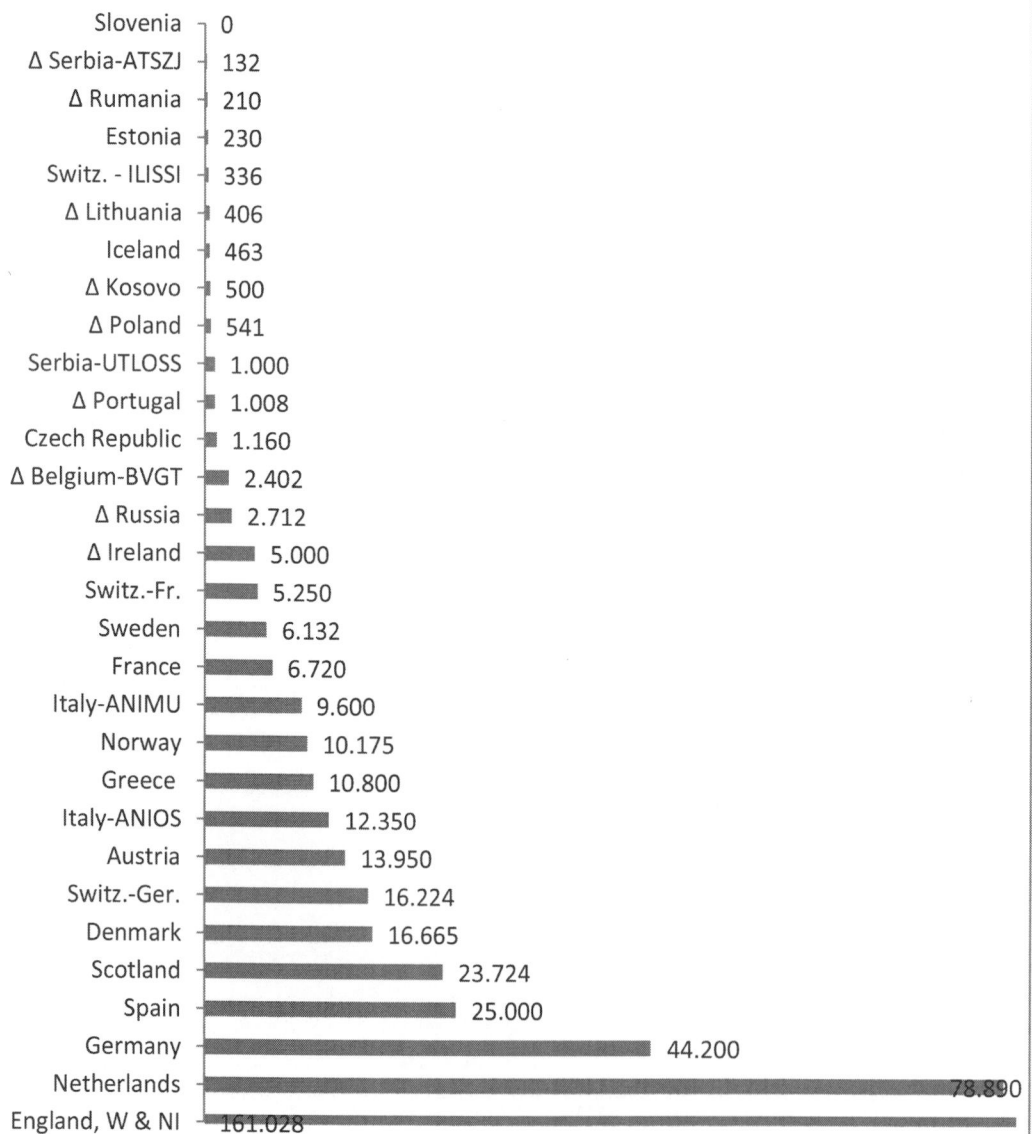

Slovenia	0
Δ Serbia-ATSZJ	132
Δ Rumania	210
Estonia	230
Switz. - ILISSI	336
Δ Lithuania	406
Iceland	463
Δ Kosovo	500
Δ Poland	541
Serbia-UTLOSS	1.000
Δ Portugal	1.008
Czech Republic	1.160
Δ Belgium-BVGT	2.402
Δ Russia	2.712
Δ Ireland	5.000
Switz.-Fr.	5.250
Sweden	6.132
France	6.720
Italy-ANIMU	9.600
Norway	10.175
Greece	10.800
Italy-ANIOS	12.350
Austria	13.950
Switz.-Ger.	16.224
Denmark	16.665
Scotland	23.724
Spain	25.000
Germany	44.200
Netherlands	78.890
England, W & NI	161.028

Not included: Finland (does not have a set rate for each interpreter member)

Δ New association since last survey in 2007

1.12 REGISTRY OF INTERPRETERS

A registry or a registration authority is an organization which has the responsibility to register and maintain an official database of the qualified interpreters within a region or country. The registry can be used for example by consumers of interpreting services or public authorities. The aim of the registry is not only to maintain a formal list of interpreters, but also to guarantee and ensure the qualifications of the interpreters who are registered. The establishment of registries has been the newest European trend in the development of the sign language interpreter profession.

Of all the 42 respondents 15 report to have a formal registry for interpreters: Austria, Belgium (Flanders & Wallonia), Cyprus, Czech Republic, England Wales & NI, Estonia, Finland, Hungary, Netherlands, Norway, Poland, Romania, Scotland, Slovenia and Switzerland-Italian region. Figure 1.8 illustrates the countries and regions with a registry and the number of registered interpreters. Poland is not included in figure 1.8 because it just established a registry, and the numbers of interpreters to be registered is still unknown. In Belgium-Flanders it is also unknown how many are registered. In Finland the number of registered interpreters is reported to be between 750 and 800. In England, Wales & Northern Ireland there are 237 trainee interpreters registered next to the 737 interpreters.

Of these 15 registries only Austria, Belgium (Wallonia), and Scotland have the registry as part of their national interpreter association. The Czech Republic and the Italian region of Switzerland indicate that their registry is part of another organization. In the Czech Republic the registry is not independent, but is part of an umbrella organization called ASNEP, is an agency which provides interpreting services. The aim is to create an independent registry in the Czech Republic in the future.

All the other countries have an independent registry. All the registries, with the exception of those in Cyprus and Belgium-Wallonia, have a prerequisite that the interpreter must have passed an exam or must be qualified as an interpreter by an official educational program. In Cyprus the interpreter must have permission from the board of the Deaf federation and have attended a special seminar through the ministry of education (the latter still needs to be installed). In the Czech Republic and the Netherlands the registered interpreters also have to be enrolled in continuing education in order to maintain registration. Belgium-Flanders mentions that their registration only consists of a governmental agency noting all the interpreters, but there are no further consequences attached. Hungary in addition mentions that a criminal record check is done before the registration is finalized and 300 hours of interpreting must be completed within the three years prior to registration. In Belgium-Wallonia the interpreters also agree to the complaint procedure when registering.

In Finland there is no official nationwide interpreter certification system. Upon graduation trained interpreters join an informal register jointly maintained by non-profit organizations. Once an interpreter is registered, the interpreter is free to work as an interpreter. According to SVT, this current register is not officially monitored and the individual interpreters' skills and work experience are not considered.

Some registries are online on the internet. Appendix 2, 'Registry of Interpreters', lists the above data in detail as well as the web addresses of the registries.

**Fig. 1.8 Number of registered interpreters
in those countries & regions with a registry**

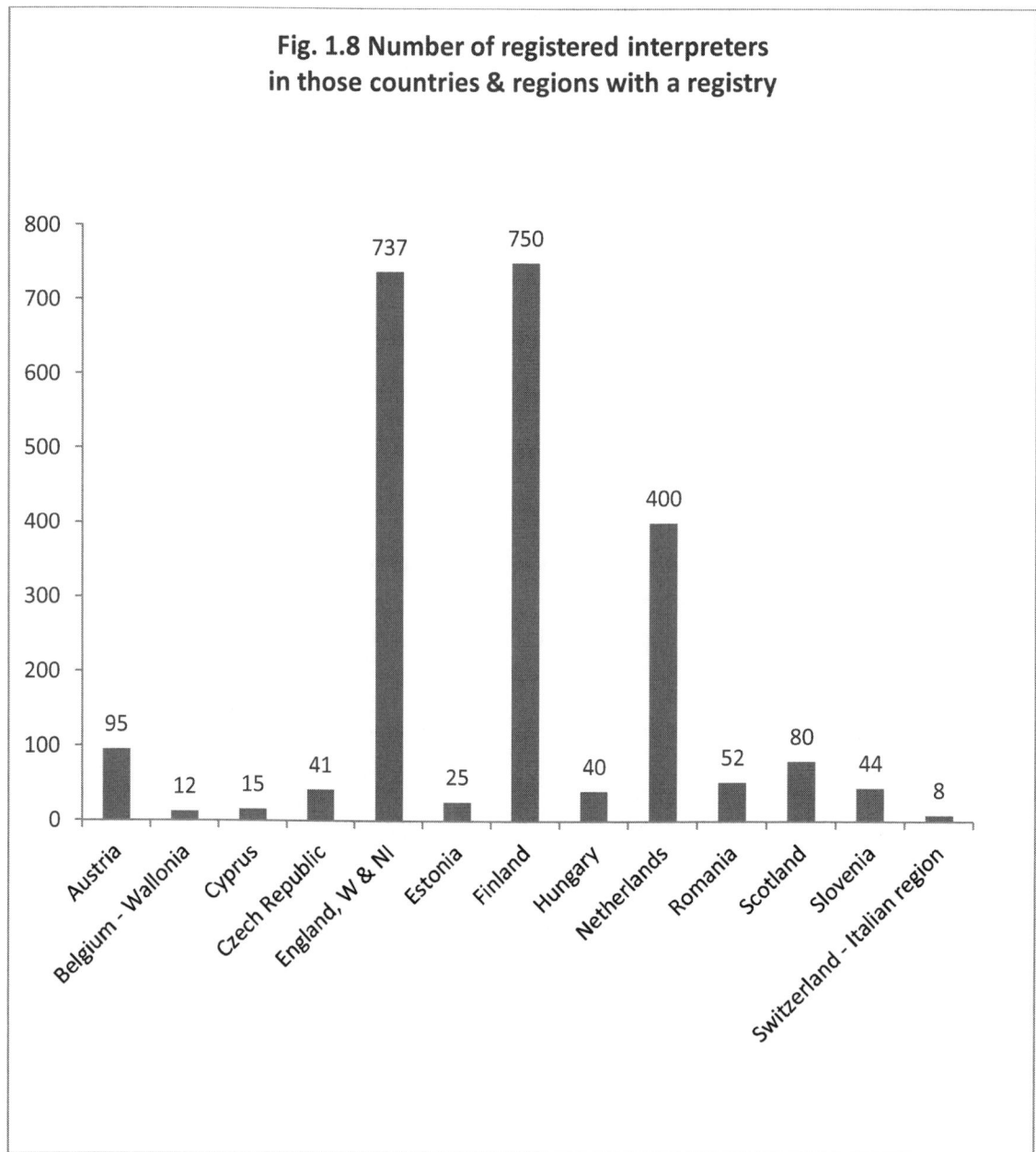

Note: Belgium-Flanders and Poland have a registry but are not included in fig. 1.8 because the number of registered interpreters is not available.

PART 2 – EDUCATION

2.1   EDUCATIONAL PROGRAMS

Historically, interpreting programs for sign language interpreters have slowly developed from a short training of a few months, to the current programs, which in most cases have a minimum of two years. There are currently more than 65 training programs for sign language interpreters in Europe (figure 2.1). The programs vary per country and language region, from very short temporary courses to five year programs and from no degree to a MA degree.

Some of the programs not only educate sign language interpreters. For example, in the Czech Republic 'Deaf Studies' focuses on sign language linguistics and pedagogy. Within 'Deaf Studies' a specialization can be taken to become a sign language interpreter. Currently preparations are taking place to establish a MA program for sign language interpreters in the Czech Republic.

There are also educational programs which have entry exams to select the students, such as in Finland. Only a maximum of 60 students per year are admitted to the program. The respondent from Russia mentions a joint project held with Finland (Humak University of Applied Sciences, Kuopio), Petrozavodsk State Pedagogical University and the Moscow center for Deaf Studies and Bilingual Education. This project resulted in the graduation of 14 interpreters. A full time MA program for Russian Sign Language Interpreters at the Moscow Linguistic University was planned to start in September 2012.

In Spain the vast majority of interpreters are trained at the over 50 centers that offer the two year program 'Ciclo superior de técnico de interpretación de lengua de signos'. The 'Master in Teaching and Interpreting Sign Language' at the University of Valladolid is for already qualified sign language interpreters and is the first Spanish program at university level.

In Denmark and the Netherlands it is a prerequisite to have a degree from the interpreting program in order to work and receive payment from the respective governments.

2.2   COUNTRIES AND REGIONS WITHOUT A PROGRAM

Albania, Belgium-Wallonia, Bosnia & Herzegovina, Croatia, Cyprus, Greece, Italy, Malta, Serbia, Switzerland (French & Italian region) and Ukraine are the countries which participated in the survey which have no officially established permanent interpreter training program.

All across Europe, there is a vast diversity in interpreter training programs, even in those countries that have no official training program.

In Albania, Bosnia-Herzegovina and Malta the interpreters are trained by the Deaf association. The Serbian respondent from ATSZJ reports:

> *"Since 2002 the Association of Deaf and Hard of Hearing of Serbia annually organizes a seminar of Sign Serbian, which lasts 7 days, and the committee appointed by that association (one deaf, one hard of hearing and two specialists) decide on who will get the certificate that entitles a person to work as a sign language interpreter. ATSZJ does not have permanent training for SLI neither a formal curriculum. So far Association of Serbian Sign Language Interpreters organized just three two-day trainings for interpreters within one project. Trainers were experienced sign language interpreters and the aspects covered*

in those trainings were Sign language competence, Spoken language competence, Interpreting skills & techniques, Ethics/Professional conduct, Social competences, Cultural awareness but all at a basic level. A total of 20 interpreters participated in the training."

Croatia is very active in training sign language interpreters at DODIR, the association for Deaf-blind people. At DODIR the students enroll in a two year sign language course, followed by a two year interpreting course. In Malta the interpreters must have a degree in a related area and are then trained by the Deaf association, which is supported by the linguistics department at the University of Malta. In Serbia there are some subjects at the university within special education and rehabilitation or the interpreter association provides a course for those who want to become an interpreter. In the French part of Switzerland there was a program at the University of Geneva which has now terminated. Plans are on the way to start a new program in 2013 or in 2014. In Italy the first permanent program is starting in 2012 at the University of Venice. In addition, there is a private school in Rome and also the Italian Deaf Association (ENS) is running a course. In Belgium-Wallonia negotiations are taking place with the public authorities to establish a formal education. ABILS, the sign language interpreter association in Wallonia, provides continuing education courses for experienced interpreters and is in the process of setting up a mentoring program.

2.3   NEW PROGRAMS

Since the last publication in 2008, new programs have been established in Belgium-Flanders, Lithuania, and Poland. At the Lessius University of Applies Sciences, Flemish Sign Language is one of third languages the BA students can chose within Applied Linguistics. Following the BA the students can continue their MA in interpreting. The program in Lithuania is the first formal education for sign language interpreters in Lithuania and it is taught as a full time three year program with a BA degree. The education in Poland is a post graduate study of 1.5 years and is directed at Polish Sign Language.

The Ukraine did not participate in the last survey, therefore the data cannot be compared. However the Ukraine did participate in the current 2012 survey and they report that they do not have a permanent program but a temporary program, which is conducted by the Training and Rehabilitation Center of the Ukrainian Society of the Deaf since 2008. This program is licensed by the Ministry of Education and Science, Youth and Sport of the Ukraine. Entry in the ITC and ATC is once or twice a year, the training accepts a maximum of 30 people. Graduates receive a state-recognized certificate, which gives them the right to interpret.

2.4   LENGTH OF THE PROGRAM

All the current formal interpreter programs have a duration of one year or more . Comparing to the last 2007 survey, changes can be seen in the duration of the existing programs. Many programs have changed into a BA degree, increasing the study duration.

The majority of the countries in Eastern Europe do not have a formal education for sign language interpreters. The programs which are available are temporary and short courses, such as a week or a month. The earlier courses for sign language interpreters in other European countries started as a short term programs. Now these all have changed into longer and permanent programs, such as the program in Scotland at Heriot Watt University, which recently changed from a two to a four year program.

An example which dates longer back is the program in the Netherlands. The first program was nine months and intended for children of Deaf parents or people active in the Deaf community who knew sign language. It is now a four year BA program.

2.5   CURRICULA

In 2011 the European Forum of Sign Language of Interpreters (efsli) started a new project aimed at designing a model curriculum for sign language interpreter training programs. Efsli had received numerous enquiries from European countries and regions without an educational program on the content of a curriculum. In addition, the existing programs in Europe continue to improve their program to meet the consumer's demands. In order to design a model curriculum, efsli researched the existing educational programs through a European survey. The results were presented in a first report (Calle, 2012a). Next, two working seminars were organized, with a third one to be held in 2013, where interpreter educators, trainers and administrators participate to map out the main parts of the curriculum. The final model curriculum will be presented by efsli in 2013.

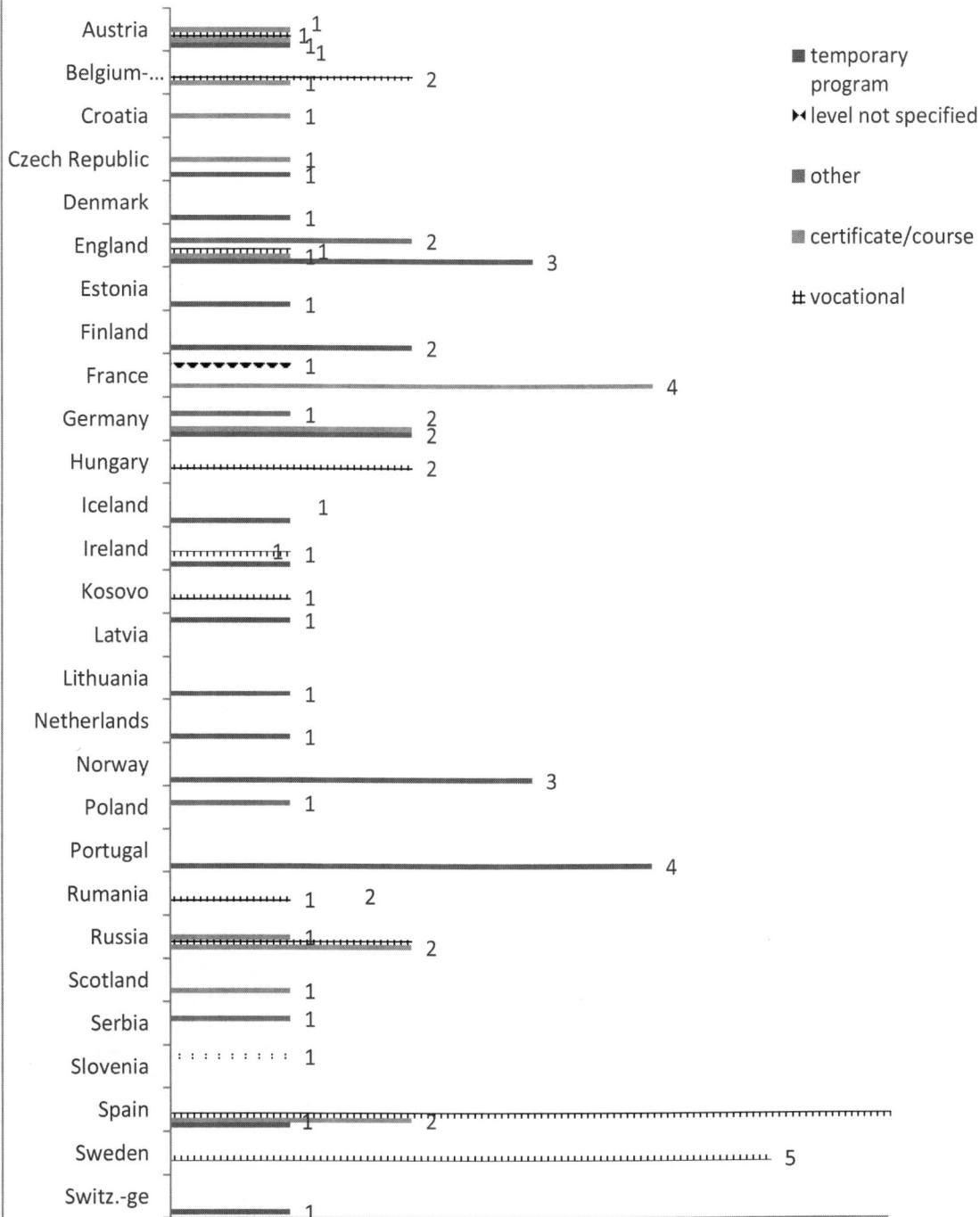

Fig. 2.1: Number of interpreter educational programs

Fig. 2.2: Overview of sign language interpreter training programs in Europe

COUNTRY	PROGRAM	LENGTH OF PROGRAM	STUDENTS ENROLLED	PART TIME / FULL TIME	DEGREE
Austria	University Graz, Translation Study, MA	5 years	~ 40	FT	BA & MA
	GESDO – Linz	3 years	15	FT	Exam
	OEGSDV – Achtung Fertig Los (AFL)	1.5 years	13	PT	Vocational
Belgium-Flanders	Lessius – Antwerp	5 years	29	FT	MA
	CVO Crescendo - Mechelen	4 years	50	PT	Vocational
	VSPW - Gent	4 years	37	PT	Vocational
Czech Republic	Czech Chamber of sign language Interpreters: certificate program	3.5 years	30 – 40	PT	Certificate
	Charles University, Prague – Faculty of Philosophy & Arts	3 - 4 years	3 – 7 in one year	FT	BA
Denmark	Center for tegnsprog – tolkeuddannelsen - Kopenhagen & Arhus	3.5 years	400 since 1988	FT	BA (from 2013 on)
England, Wales & Northern Ireland	University of Bristol ➢ *looking to establish an MSc interpreting unit (1 year full-time/2 years part-time)* http://www.bris.ac.uk/deaf/english /postgraduate/msc/units.html)	3 years, undergr. (last course 2012-2013)	Unknown	FT	BSc (Hons)
	University of Wolverhampton: (Hons) Interpreting British Sign Language (BSL)/English	3 years	85	FT	BA
	Interpreting BSL/English plus Foundation (for students with no previous sign language skills)	4 years		FT	BA
	University of Central Lancashire	2 years - graduate	Unknown	PT	Graduate diploma
		2 years, postgrad.		PT	PGDip
		1 year		PT	MA
	NVQ level 6 Diploma in BSL/English interpreting – delivered by various centers		Unknown	PT	Vocational
Estonia	University of Tartu (Eesti viipekeele tõlk)	3 years	16 students every 3	FT	BA
Finland	Diaconia, University of Applied Sciences – Turku	4 years	129	FT	BA
	HUMAK, University of Applied Sciences (Helsinki & Kuopio)	4 years	221	FT	BA
France	Master in interpretation French/French Sign Language, French Sign Language/French – Paris	2 years	25	PT	MA
	University Paris 8 – Saint Denis	2 years	25	FT	MA
	Lille	2 years	25	FT	MA
	Rouen Université	2 years		FT	
	Toulouse, university	3 years	10	FT	MA
Germany	University of Hamburg	3.5 years	~ 65	FT	BA

COUNTRY	PROGRAM	LENGTH OF PROGRAM	STUDENTS ENROLLED	PART TIME / FULL TIME	DEGREE
	Westsächsische Hochschule Zwickau	4 years	74	FT	Diploma
	Hochschule Magdeburg	3.5 years	~ 60	FT	BA
	Humboldt Universitat – Berlin	2 years		FT	MA
	Hochschule – Fresenius	2.5 years	27	PT	MA
Hungary	Sign Language Interpreter Training of ELTE BGGyF (Special Education for Handicap) – Budapest	8 months	10 – 11	PT	Vocational
	National Association of the Deaf (SINOSZ) - Budapest	2 years	12	PT	Vocational
Iceland	University of Iceland, Dept. of Sign Language Linguistics and Interpretation	3 years	Currently 6-8	FT	BA
Ireland	Centre for Deaf Studies, Trinity College - Dublin	4 years	28	FT	BA
	Centre for Language Studies - Galway	Starts in 2014	5 students in preparation course studying ISL language at British L6NVQ (L8 in Ireland)	PT	British Level 6 National Vocational Qualification Diploma in Sign Language Interpreting (=Level 8 in Ireland - degree level of complexity)
Kosovo	Prishtina	3 years	22	PT	Vocational
Latvia	Sociālās integrācijas valsts aģentūra – Jurmala	Last program in	14	PT	Vocational
Lithuania	College - Professional Bachelor in Philology, draftsman of the translator – Vilnius	3 years	100	FT	BA
Netherlands	University of Applied Sciences – Utrecht	4 years	207	PT & FT	BA (possibility to add MA Deaf Studies)
Norway	Høgskolen i Oslo og Akershus - Oslo	3 years	~25 p. year	FT	BA
	Høgskolen i Sør-Trøndelag – Trondheim	3 years	~25 p. year	FT	BA
	Høgskolen i Bergen - Bergen	3 years	~25 p. year	FT	BA
Poland	"Polish Sign Language" Postgraduate Studies – Warsaw	1.5 years	30 – 35	PT weekend	Post graduate
Portugal	Tradução e Interpretação de Língua Gestual Portuguesa - Setúbal	3 years	26	FT	BA - Licenciatura - 180 ECTS
	Tradução e Interpretação em Língua Gestual Portuguesa (day time) - Porto	3 years	30	FT	BA - Licenciatura - 180 ECTS
	Tradução e Interpretação em Língua Gestual Portuguesa (night time) – Porto	3 years	Unknown	FT	BA - Licenciatura - 180 ECTS
	Língua Gestual Portuguesa – Ramo da Interpretação - Coimbra	3 years	49	FT	BA - Licenciatura - 180 ECTS

COUNTRY	PROGRAM	LENGTH OF PROGRAM	STUDENTS ENROLLED	PART TIME / FULL TIME	DEGREE
Romania	"Curs de Inițiere în Limbaj Mimico - Gestual" - Course in "Introduction in Sign Language" , University, Cluj Napoca	3 months	37	PT	Vocational
Russia	Leningrad Rehabilitation Centre (signed Russian, distant learning), since 1965		20 per year	PT	Vocational
	Galina Zaitseva Moscow Centre for Deaf Studies and Bilingual Education, since 1993		Varies	PT	Centre's certificate & RASLI Assessment Commission's certificate
	Moscow State Pegadogical University		16 in 2009	PT	MA
	Russian State Social University	1 year	130	PT	MA (level of RSL varies)
	Novosibirsk State Social University – Novosibirsk	4 years	5	FT	Vocational
Scotland	School of Languages, Heriot-Watt University	4 years	Unknown	FT	MA
Serbia	The Association of Deaf and Hard of Hearing of Serbia – Belgrade	7 days	40 – 50 persons in one group	6 hrs per day	No level
Slovenia	Preparatory program for the certificate of national professional qualification of SLI	1 year	~10 (not every year)	PT	
Spain	Vocational training (over 50 different centres), Ciclo superior de técnico de interpretación de lengua de signos	2 years	~ 500	FT (mainly) & PT	Vocational
	Degree in Translating and Interpreting (LSC track) at the Pompeu Fabra University - Barcelona	4 years	20	FT	BA
	Master in Teaching and Interpreting Sign Language at the University of Valladolid – Valladolid	1 year	12	FT	MA
	Master in Deaf Community, education and sign language at the University of Barcelona (UB) – Barcelona	1 year	~ 10	FT	MA
Sweden	Strömbäcks folkhögskola – Umeå	4 years	Varies	FT	Vocational
	Fellingsbro folkhögskola – Örebro	4 years	Varies	FT	Vocational
	Önnestads folkhögskola – Önnestad	4 years	Varies	FT	Vocational
	Härnösands folkhögskola – Härnösand	4 years	Varies	first year distance , there after full time at the	Vocational
	Nordiska folkhögskola – Kungälv	4 years	Varies	FT	Vocational
Switzerland – German	HfH Hochschule für Heilpädagogik, Studiengang GSD – Zurich	3 – 4 years	10-20	FT – 3 yrs PT – 4 yrs	BA

Fig. 2.3: Number of educational programs in Europe per educational level

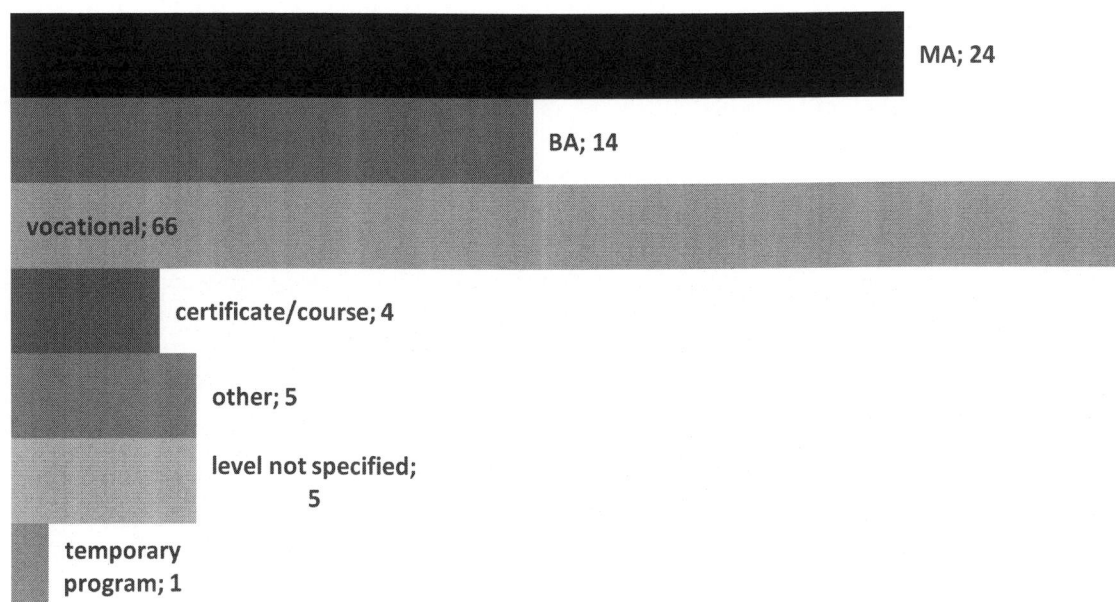

MA; 24

BA; 14

vocational; 66

certificate/course; 4

other; 5

level not specified; 5

temporary program; 1

Note: UK and Spain report to have several centers with a specific program. The total number of these centers are not incorporated in the above graph, but are counted as one.

2.6 STUDENTS ENROLLED IN THE INTERPRETER TRAINING PROGRAM

Figure 2.2 provides a total overview of the education of sign language interpreters and specifically on the number of students enrolled. There are 25 countries and regions which are able provide the number of students currently enrolled in the educational programs for sign language interpreters (figure 2.4). Not all respondents were able to provide this. Additional information, where possible, was collected through direct contact with the programs. Otherwise, the cell in table 2.2 states 'unknown' or it contains a description provided by the respondent.

Figure 2.4 shows the total current number of students in 25 countries studying to become a sign language interpreter, with a total of 2592. In the calculation the lowest number provided by the respondent is used. For example, Serbia indicated 40 to 50 persons, the number 40 is used in the graph.

In England, Wales & Northern Ireland the respondent was not able to provide the exact number of students for the programs, especially not for the NVQ level 6 Diploma in BSL/English interpreting delivered by various centers. The only specific data was provided by the University of Wolverhampton.

The students in the past temporary programs are not included in figure 2.4. For example in the Ukraine a temporary educational program has run in the past as well as a temporary training in the French and Italian region of Switzerland.

Figure 2.5 indicates the number of students which have graduated from the interpreter training programs from the start of the program on. Only the numbers are incorporated in the figure of the countries that were able to give an estimate and which were not in contradiction with other numbers provided. Spain has the largest number of graduates, more than 5,000.

It seems harder for the respondents to give an exact number on the graduates when the country is large or when there is more than one program in the country. The smaller countries were able to give more exact numbers on the number of graduates. The total number of graduates, of the 19 countries and regions that could give an estimate, is 8332.

Fig. 2.4: Number of students currently enrolled in an interpreter training program

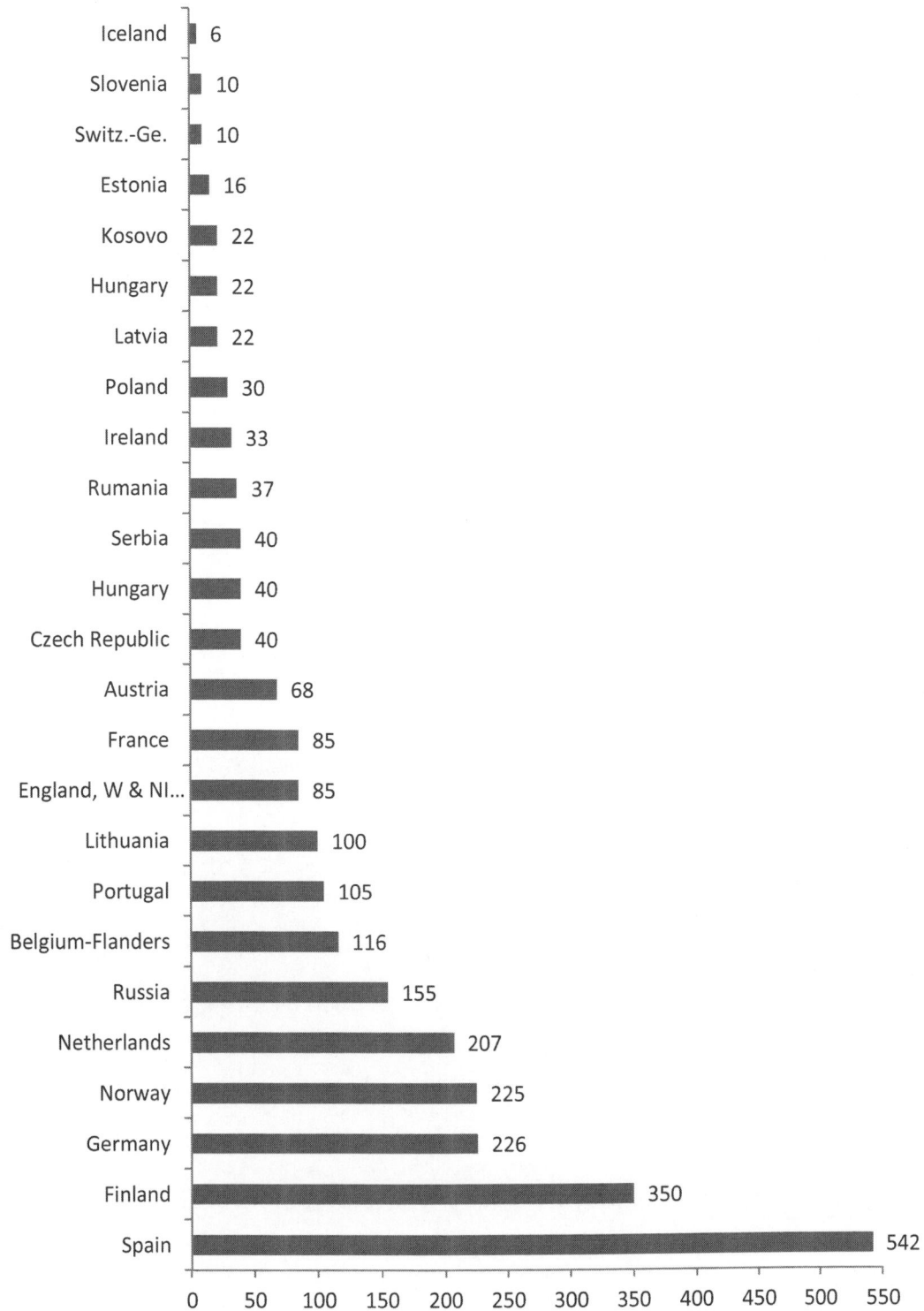

Iceland	6
Slovenia	10
Switz.-Ge.	10
Estonia	16
Kosovo	22
Hungary	22
Latvia	22
Poland	30
Ireland	33
Rumania	37
Serbia	40
Hungary	40
Czech Republic	40
Austria	68
France	85
England, W & NI...	85
Lithuania	100
Portugal	105
Belgium-Flanders	116
Russia	155
Netherlands	207
Norway	225
Germany	226
Finland	350
Spain	542

Fig. 2.5: Total number of students who graduated from an interpreter training program

Czech Republic	10
Kosovo	11
Latvia	17
Rumania	34
Iceland	37
Switz.-Ge.	60
Lithuania	60
Austria	70
Poland	70
Ireland	92
Serbia	100
Ukraine	121
Hungary	200
France	380
Belgium-Flanders	400
Denmark	400
Portugal	470
Norway	800
Spain	5000

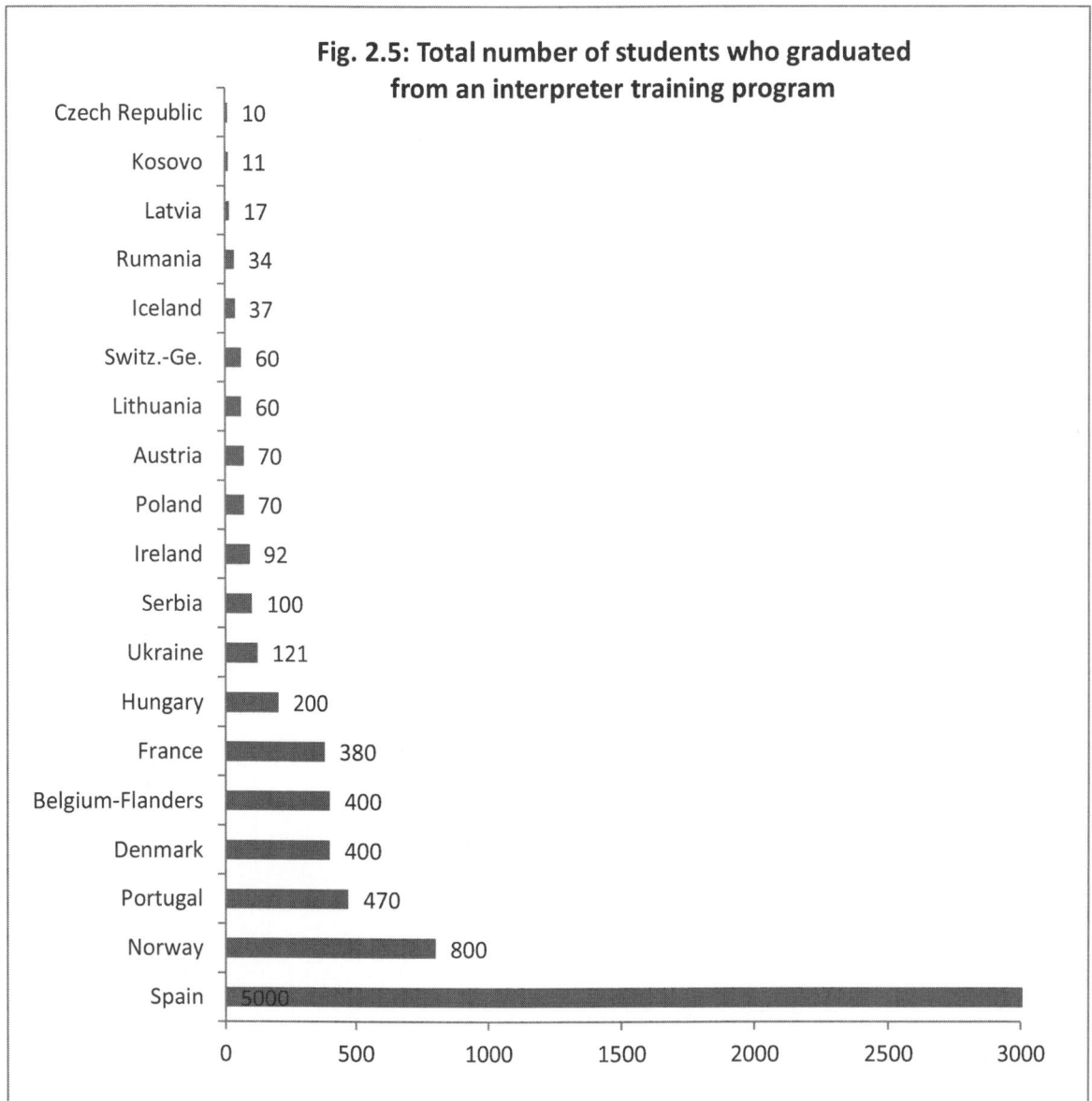

Figure 2.5: Additional comments

If countries gave a number range, the lower number was used in the figure.

- Spain: estimated more than 5000
- Norway: the 800 is an estimate
- Russia: not included in the graph, only mentioned graduates from one program: "in RSL 26 graduates, MSPU, 2010 and 2011 part time"
- Ukraine: ITC - 25; ATC - 96
- Netherlands: 117 till 1997 & 143 from the new BA program

PART 3 – EMPLOYMENT

3.1 INTERPRETERS CURRENTLY WORKING

Part 1 gave an estimation (figure 1.5) of the total number of currently working sign language interpreters based on the membership numbers of the national associations of sign language interpreters. The respondents were also asked how many interpreters were currently working in their country or region. Figure 3.1 provides the result of this question.

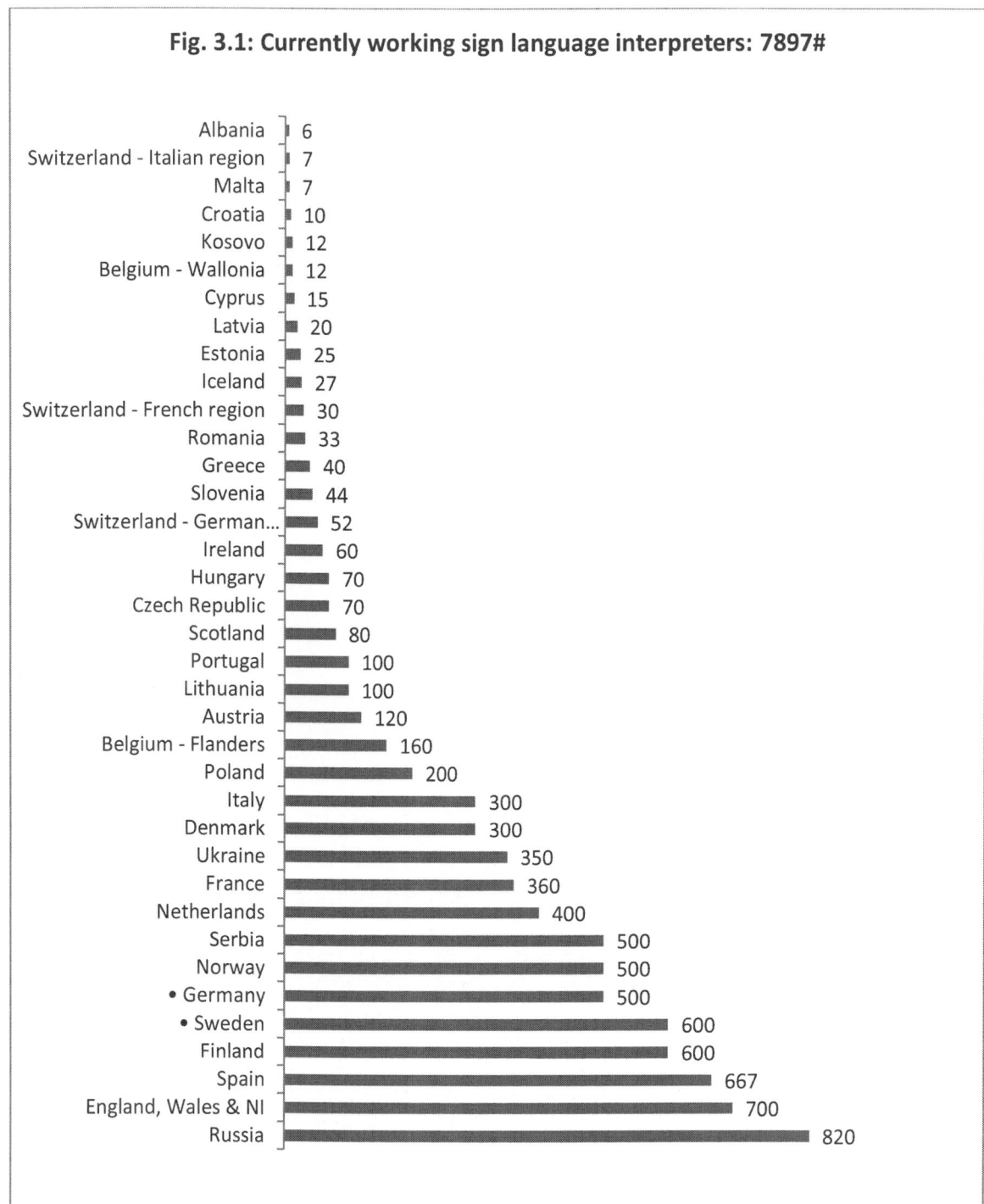

Fig. 3.1: Currently working sign language interpreters: 7897#

Albania	6
Switzerland - Italian region	7
Malta	7
Croatia	10
Kosovo	12
Belgium - Wallonia	12
Cyprus	15
Latvia	20
Estonia	25
Iceland	27
Switzerland - French region	30
Romania	33
Greece	40
Slovenia	44
Switzerland - German...	52
Ireland	60
Hungary	70
Czech Republic	70
Scotland	80
Portugal	100
Lithuania	100
Austria	120
Belgium - Flanders	160
Poland	200
Italy	300
Denmark	300
Ukraine	350
France	360
Netherlands	400
Serbia	500
Norway	500
• Germany	500
• Sweden	600
Finland	600
Spain	667
England, Wales & NI	700
Russia	820

 # Not included: Bosnia Herzegovina. The total number for Sweden and Germany are taken from the 2007 survey.

• Data used from 2007 survey

In figure 1.5 the total number of sign language interpreters was estimated on the basis of the percentage of interpreters which is a member of the interpreter association. The number of interpreters in figure 1.5 is the number of sign language interpreters in the country or region, but it does not indicate the actual working number of interpreters. The estimated number of currently working interpreters is shown in figure 3.1 with a total of 7897 interpreters.

Bosnia-Herzegovina, Sweden and Germany were unable to provide a number of working interpreters. The numbers for Sweden and Germany used in figure 3.1 are from the 2007 survey. Bosnia-Herzegovina did not participate in the 2007 survey and therefore no number is used. The majority of the countries with a large number of interpreters state that the total number provided is an estimate. The countries with a smaller number of interpreters are able to provide a more precise number. Spain also mentions that FILSE carried out a survey with the result showing that there are 667 working interpreters, but they are assuming that there are more than their survey indicates.

Russia has the highest number of interpreters, followed by England, Wales & NI, Spain and Finland. Albania, the Italian region of Switzerland and Malta have the lowest number of interpreters. The ten interpreters mentioned by Croatia are the interpreters working for DODIR, the organization for deaf-blind persons in Croatia. There are more sign language interpreters working in Croatia, but no data could be provided.

3.2   LACK OF INTERPRETERS

In the 2005 publication, all 29 respondents reported a lack of sign language interpreters in their country, except ANIOS, one of the two associations in Italy, and the Italian speaking part of Switzerland. In this 2012 survey the 41 responses show a different result.

Six of the respondents, namely Italy (ANIOS), Latvia, Portugal, and all the three regions in Switzerland state there is no lack of interpreters in their countries or regions. ANIOS reports that this is due to the fact that Deaf persons must pay for the interpreting services themselves and therefore only book an interpreter for the most important meetings. Therefore the current number of interpreters can fulfill these requests. Portugal gives a similar reason, there are only few requests and these can be met by the current number of interpreters. In the French region of Switzerland three percent of the requests cannot be met, which is not considered a lack of interpreters by the respondent. The other regions of Switzerland report a similar situation.

Denmark, Finland, Iceland, Italy (ANIMU), Lithuania, Netherlands, Serbia, Sweden and England, Wales & Northern Ireland indicate that they do not know if there is a lack of interpreters in their country.

All the other 26 respondents report a lack of interpreters. For example, Albania and Malta, respectively have 6 and 7 interpreters, who do not all work full time. In Belgium-Flanders, the majority of the interpreters have an additional job next to working as an interpreter, due to the insufficient payment they receive as an interpreter. Insufficient payment is also cited by Bosnia-Herzegovina as the cause of interpreter shortage. Estonia and Slovenia indicate that only larger cities have sufficient interpreters. Other countries, such as Poland, mention the lack of interpreters within specific domains such as in academic and educational settings.

In some countries official research has been done on the number of interpreters that is needed to fill the shortage of interpreters. In the Netherlands this was published in a report covering the consequences of the future recognition of sign language in the Netherlands.4 One of the consequences is the right of Deaf people to sign language interpreting services. This right will then increases the demand for sign language interpreters. Sign language is still not recognized in the Netherlands, and as a resulted the predicted demand for 800 interpreters has not come true.

3.3 NUMBER OF WORKING INTERPRETERS: 2001 & 2004 & 2007 & 2012

In the first 2001 report, a total of 21 countries reported on the number of interpreters. In figure 3.2 a comparison is made between the same 21 countries in 2004, 2007, and 2012. In 2001 there were 3153, in 2004 4155, in 2007 4766 interpreters and in 2012 5431 working in the same 21 countries. The only country that is not included in the 2007 numbers is Slovenia, since it did not participate in the 2007 survey.

The increase of the total number of interpreters in the 21 countries during these 11 years is 2278 interpreters, 72 percent. Large increases from 2001 to 2012 can be found in Denmark, England, Wales & Northern Ireland, Finland, France, the Netherlands and Norway. Some countries such as Portugal and Spain show a decrease in the number of interpreters. Germany and Sweden were unable to give a current number of interpreters, so a comparison with earlier years cannot be made. To calculate the total number, the numbers of the 2007 survey are used for Germany (500) and Sweden (600).

4. Report *Meer dan een Gebaar,* 1997: Report of the Commission on the recognition of Dutch Sign Language

Fig. 3.2: Number of working interpreters compared: 2001, 2004, 2007, 2012 - 19 countries (2001 report)

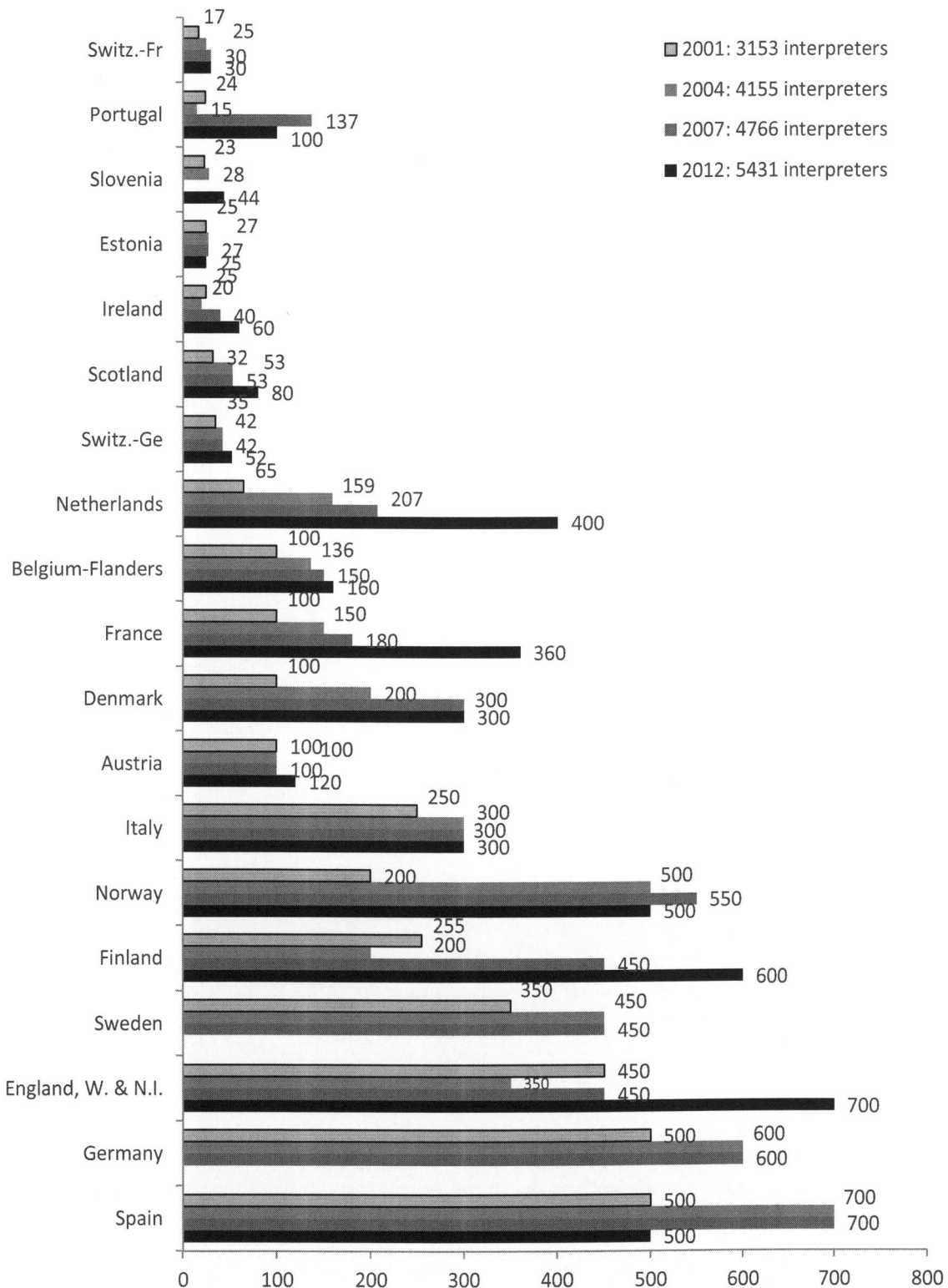

Legend:
- 2001: 3153 interpreters
- 2004: 4155 interpreters
- 2007: 4766 interpreters
- 2012: 5431 interpreters

Country	2001	2004	2007	2012
Switz.-Fr	17	25	30	30
Portugal	24	15	137	100
Slovenia	23	28	25	44
Estonia	27	27	25	25
Ireland	20	40	60	
Scotland	32	53	53	80
Switz.-Ge	35	42	42	52
Netherlands	65	159	207	400
Belgium-Flanders	100	136	150	160
France	100	150	180	360
Denmark	100	200	300	300
Austria	100	100	100	120
Italy	250	300	300	300
Norway	200	500	550	500
Finland	255	200	450	600
Sweden	350	450	450	
England, W. & N.I.	450	350	450	700
Germany	500	600	600	
Spain	500	700	700	500

41

3.4   DEAF SIGN LANGUAGE USERS

Figure 3.3 shows an estimate of the number of Deaf sign language users in 36 countries and regions, (1,087,994). The respondents from Croatia and Kosovo were unable to give the number of Deaf sign language users in their country. DODIR, the association for Deafblind persons in Croatia, says there are 350 Deafblind sign language users in Croatia. Some countries, such as Slovenia, undertook national demographic studies and are able to present exact results. The majority of the countries are unable to provide precise data, but show an indication based on for example services or Deaf persons enrolled in education. Serbia mentions that the data of 30,000 was provided by the national deaf association in Serbia.

In the 2007 survey 29 countries in Europe participated with a total of 627,190 Deaf persons who use sign language as their preferred mode of communication.

The European Union of the Deaf (EUD) published the results from this survey and publication 'Sign Language Interpreting in Europe, 2012 edition' in their newest publication 'Sign Language Legislation in the European Union'. EUD focuses on the countries within the European Union and has therefore limited the publication of the numbers to the EU countries (Wheatley & Pabsch, 2012; p. 20), resulting in a total of 802,324 within the EU.

3.5   DEAF SIGN LANGUAGE USERS PER INTERPRETER

In total there are approximately 1 million sign language users and over 7000 sign language interpreters in Europe. In figure 3.4 a total of 35 countries provide a number of Deaf sign language users (1,087,944) and working sign language interpreters (7875). The figure indicates the number of Deaf sign language users per interpreter in the given country. The average number of interpreters per country is 235.

The highest number of sign language users per interpreter is in Romania (745), Portugal (600), Ukraine (429) and Germany (400). There are also countries such as Norway and Finland, which have respectively 5 and 8 sign language users per interpreter.

Fig. 3.3: Deaf sign language users: 1,087,994#

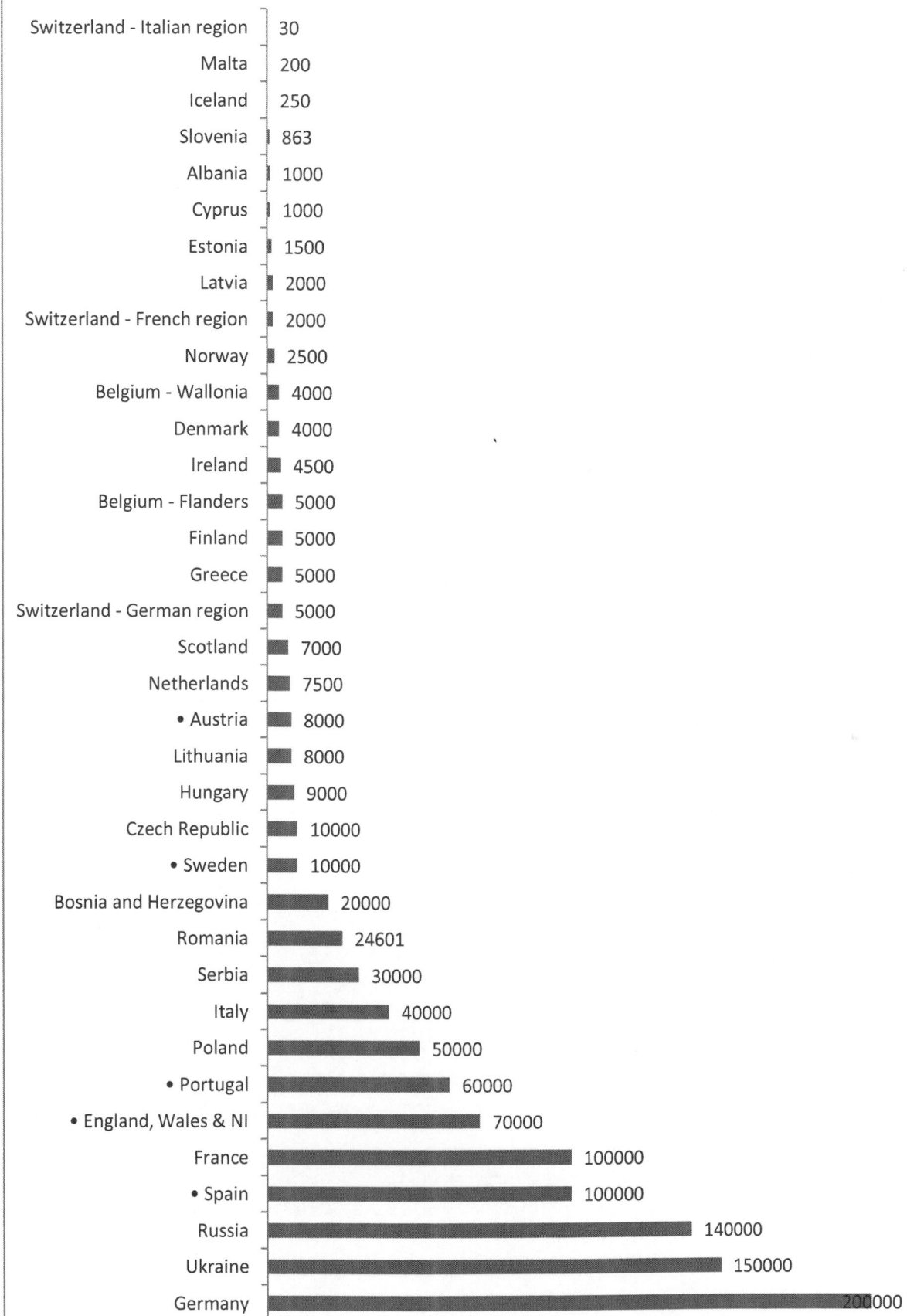

Switzerland - Italian region	30
Malta	200
Iceland	250
Slovenia	863
Albania	1000
Cyprus	1000
Estonia	1500
Latvia	2000
Switzerland - French region	2000
Norway	2500
Belgium - Wallonia	4000
Denmark	4000
Ireland	4500
Belgium - Flanders	5000
Finland	5000
Greece	5000
Switzerland - German region	5000
Scotland	7000
Netherlands	7500
• Austria	8000
Lithuania	8000
Hungary	9000
Czech Republic	10000
• Sweden	10000
Bosnia and Herzegovina	20000
Romania	24601
Serbia	30000
Italy	40000
Poland	50000
• Portugal	60000
• England, Wales & NI	70000
France	100000
• Spain	100000
Russia	140000
Ukraine	150000
Germany	200000

Not included Croatia & Kosovo

• Data used from 2007 survey

Fig. 3.4: Deaf sign language users per interpreter#

Switzerland - Italian region	4
Norway	5
Finland	8
Iceland	9
Denmark	13
Sweden	17
Netherlands	19
Slovenia	20
Malta	29
Belgium - Flanders	31
Estonia	60
Serbia	60
Austria	67
Cyprus	67
Switzerland - French region	67
Ireland	75
Lithuania	80
Scotland	88
Switzerland - German region	96
England, Wales & NI	100
Latvia	100
Greece	125
Hungary	129
Italy	133
Czech Republic	143
Spain	150
Albania	167
Russia	171
Poland	250
France	278
Belgium - Wallonia	333
Germany	400
Ukraine	429
Portugal	600
Romania	745

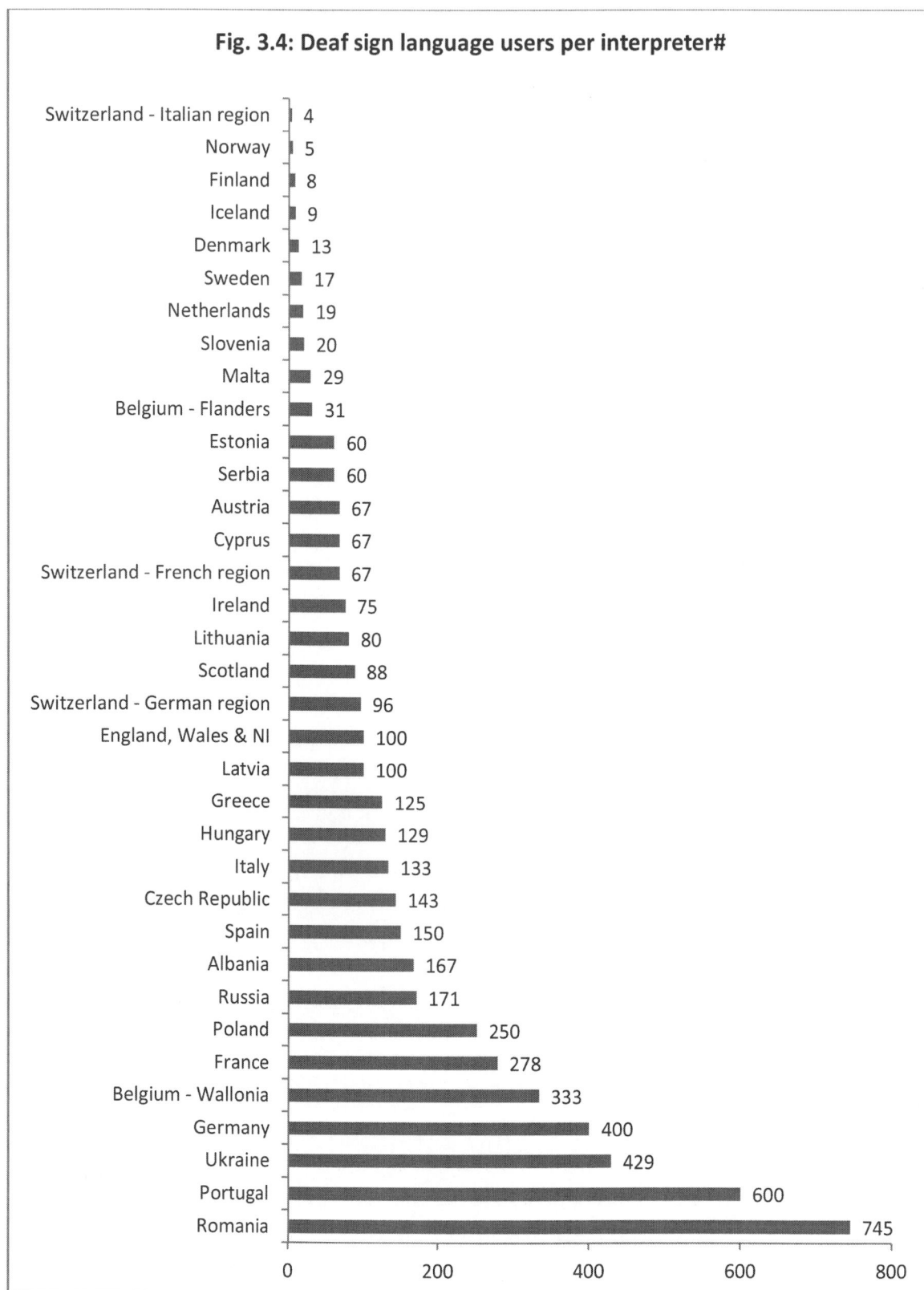

Not included Bosnia-Herzegovina, Croatia, Kosovo

3.6 THE RIGHT TO AN INTERPRETER

Each country in Europe has different rights, regulations and laws in regard to sign language interpreting. The first EU Directive on the Rights to Interpretation and Translation in criminal proceedings was adopted in October 2010 by the EU Council of Ministers.5 This directive only gives the right to an interpreter or translator in criminal proceedings and not in other settings.

In 2011 the European Forum of Sign Language Interpreters (efsli) published a report 'The Rights to Sign Language Interpreting Services when Working or Studying Abroad'. The reported showed that each country has their own rights to sign language interpreting services depending on the setting. It also shows that the majority of the countries do not allow the right to an interpreter when working or studying abroad.

The respondents from Albania, Ireland, Malta, and Serbia indicate that the Deaf persons do not have a right to an interpreter in their country. Ireland says that the Deaf person has a right to reasonable accommodation, but this does not mean automatically an interpreter. Malta clarifies that the government does provide the service, but it is not yet a legal right.

Austria, Belgium-Wallonia, Croatia, Germany, Italy, Portugal, Romania, Russia, Serbia, Sweden, Switzerland-It state that Deaf persons partially have a right to an interpreter. All the other countries indicate that the Deaf persons do have a right to an interpreter. For an overview of these rights and the legal texts, see appendix 3 'Right to an Interpreter' and the EUD publication 'Sign Language Legislation in the European Union'(2012).

---

5. http://www.consilium.europa.eu/uedocs/cms_data/docs/pressdata/en/jha/116913.pdf (last accessed 25 October 2012)

3.7   RECOGNITION OF SIGN LANGUAGE

Of the 40 countries and regions 65% have recognized sign language as an official language (fig. 3.5). The first to recognize sign language as an official language was Sweden in 1981. The most recent one is Poland in 2012. Since the last survey in 2007, eight more countries formally recognized sign language.

Country	Sign Language recognition
Sweden	1981
Finland	1995
Lithuania	1995
Portugal	1997
Czech Republic	1998
Latvia	2000, September
Greece	2001
Germany	2002
Romania	2002
Slovenia	2002
Belgium – Wallonia	2003
England, Wales & NI	2003, March
Austria	2005
France	2005
Belgium – Flanders	2006, March
Cyprus	2006
Estonia	2007, March
Spain	2007, June
Hungary	2009
Bosnia-Herzegovina	2010
Kosovo	2010
Switzerland – French region	2010
Iceland	2011
Scotland	2011
Ukraine	2011
Poland	2012
Albania	No
Croatia	No
Denmark	No
Ireland	No
Italy	No
Malta	No
Netherlands	No
Norway	No
Russia	No
Serbia	No
Switzerland – Italian & German region	No

Fig. 3.5 Sign Language recognition per country or region

3.8   INTERPRETERS: FORMS OF EMPLOYMENT

Sign language interpreters across Europe work in different forms of employment (fig. 3.6). Interpreters can all work for an agency, which is the case in 9% of the countries and regions, or work all as freelancers (14%), or a combination with mostly freelance and some for an agency (10%) or mostly for an agency and some freelance (21%).

The majority (29%) of the countries have different forms of employment (fig. 3.7b), such as for the national Deaf association (Cyprus, Malta, Spain, Ukraine), or as freelancers and paid through an agency (Czech Republic, Switzerland – German region), or for private companies (Finland, Sweden) and also interpreters who have another full time job next to interpreting (Estonia, Kosovo).

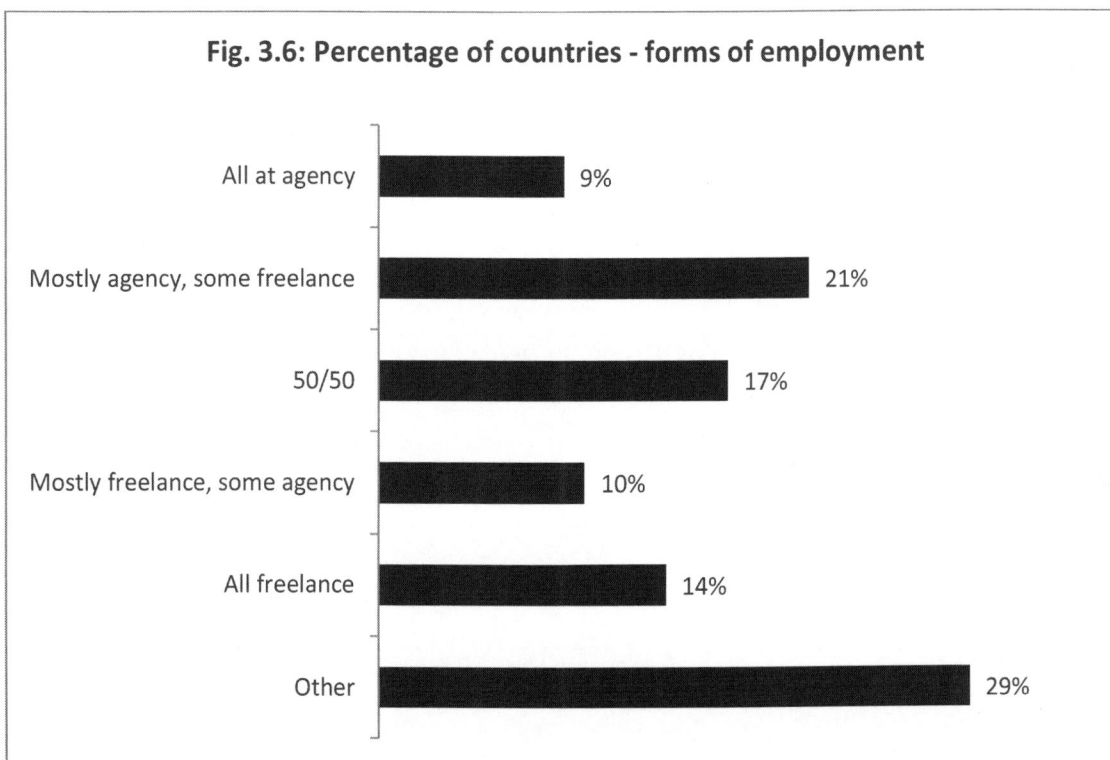

Fig. 3.6: Percentage of countries - forms of employment

- All at agency: 9%
- Mostly agency, some freelance: 21%
- 50/50: 17%
- Mostly freelance, some agency: 10%
- All freelance: 14%
- Other: 29%

All as freelancers	Mostly as freelancers, some for an agency	50% freelancers, 50% for an agency	Mostly for an agency, some as freelancers	All for an agency
Bosnia-Herzegovina	Austria	Hungary	Albania	Belgium – Wallonia
Croatia	Belgium – Flanders	Ireland	Denmark	Lithuania
Greece	Germany	Italy-ANIMU	France	Serbia - UTLOSS
Italy – ANIOS	Netherlands	Norway	Iceland	Switzerland – It.
Poland		Scotland	Latvia	
Serbia - ATSZJ		Slovenia	Portugal	
		UK	Romania	
			Russia	
			Switzerland – Fr.	

Figure 3.7a: Employment forms per country and region

Other	Namely:
Cyprus	They work under the Cyprus Deaf Federation who receives funding from the government
Czech Republic	They work mostly as freelancers, but are mostly paid by an agency. Some of them are hired by some school for the Deaf or a Centre for handicapped students.
Estonia	Mostly for agencies, but most of them have a full job other than interpreting and interpret only a small number of hours
Finland	All for agency or under a private trade name
Kosovo	There is no agency and most of the interpreters work full time
Malta	Some as freelance and some for the Deaf association
Portugal	For educational departments and some as a freelancers
Spain	In Deaf People's Associations
Sweden	Agencies, freelancers and private companies -two areas have been outsourced from the county council
Switzerland – Ge.	All for an agency but as freelancers
Ukraine	Most of interpreters are full-time employees of the Ukrainian Society of the Deaf, as well as its institutions and enterprises

Figure 3.7b: Other employment forms per country and region

3.9   RESPONSIBLE PARTY FOR THE PAYMENT OF INTERPRETING SERVICES

As stated earlier, each country in Europe has different regulations and laws in regard to sign language interpreting. The payment of the interpreting services also differs per country and per setting. The respondents were asked who is the responsible paying party for five main settings where interpreting services can be provided: employment (fig. 3.8), education (fig. 3.9), medical (fig. 3.10), legal (fig. 3.11) and theatre (fig. 3.12).

In most of the countries the government is responsible for paying the interpreting services in employment, educational, medical and legal settings. The only exception in this are the theatre settings, where in most countries the theatres pay for the interpreting services. In educational settings there are also many countries where the educational institutions pay for the interpreting services. Albania is the only country where no payment for interpreting services is available. In Kosovo there is also little provision, only in legal and educational settings.

In many countries there are restrictions on the government funding for interpreting services. The restriction is often linked to the situation and, or to a set budget per person. In the Netherlands, for example, Deaf people have a right to an interpreter 15% of their work time, and 100% in education. In addition, they have 30 hours a year for other situations. Deafblind people have a right to a total of 168 hours of interpreting services per year.

COUNTRY	Government / agency	Employer	Educa-tional program	Deaf club	Deaf person	Other	NA
Fig. 3.8: EMPLOYMENT SETTING Responsible party for the payment of the interpreting services							
Albania							X
Austria	X						
Belgium - Flanders	X						
Belgium - Wallonia	X						
Bosnia-Herzegovina	X	X					
Croatia	X						
Cyprus				X			
Czech Republic	X						
Denmark	X						
England, Wales & NI	X	X					
Estonia	X	X			X		
Finland	X	X					
France		X					
Germany	X	X			X		
Greece	X				X	X	
Hungary	X						
Iceland	X						
Ireland	X	X					
Italy - ANIMU					X		
Italy - ANIOS					X		
Kosovo							X
Latvia	X						
Lithuania						X	
Malta	X	X					
Netherlands	X						
Norway	X						
Poland	X	X			X		
Portugal		X			X		
Romania		X		X	X		
Russia	X	X		X	X	X	
Scotland	X						
Serbia - ATSZJ					X		
Serbia - UTLOSS	X			X			
Slovenia		X				X	
Spain	X			X	X		
Sweden	X						
Switzerland – Fr.	X		X				
Switzerland – Ge.	X						
Switzerland – It.	X						
Ukraine		X					

Figure 3.8

COUNTRY	Government / agency	Employer	Educational program	Deaf person	Other	NA
Fig. 3.9: EDUCATIONAL SETTING Responsible party for the payment of the interpreting services						
Albania						X
Austria	X		X			
Belgium - Flanders	X					
Belgium - Wallonia	X					
Bosnia-Herzegovina	X	X				
Croatia	X					
Cyprus	X					
Czech Republic			X			
Denmark	X					
England, Wales & NI	X					
Estonia	X	X	X	X		
Finland	X					
France	X					
Germany	X		X	X		
Greece	X	X	X	X	X	
Hungary	X					
Iceland			X			
Ireland	X		X			
Italy - ANIMU	X					
Italy – ANIOS		X	X			
Kosovo			X			
Latvia	X			X		
Lithuania					X	
Malta	X		x			
Netherlands	X					
Norway	X					
Poland			X			
Portugal	X			X		
Romania			X	X		X
Russia	X		X	X		
Scotland	X					
Serbia - ATSZJ						X
Serbia - UTLOSS			X			
Slovenia	X					
Spain			X			
Sweden			X			
Switzerland – Fr.	X					
Switzerland – Ge.	X					
Switzerland – It.	X					
Ukraine		X	X	X		

Figure 3.9

COUNTRY	Government / agency	Employer	Deaf club	Deaf person	Other	NA
Fig. 3.10: MEDICAL SETTING Responsible party for the payment of the interpreting services						
Albania						X
Austria	X					
Belgium - Flanders	X			X		
Belgium - Wallonia	X					
Bosnia-Herzegovina			X			
Croatia	X					
Cyprus			X			
Czech Republic	X					
Denmark	X					
England, Wales & NI	X					
Estonia	X	X		X		
Finland	X				X	
France				X		
Germany					X	
Greece	X				X	
Hungary	X					
Iceland	X					
Ireland	X					
Italy - ANIMU				X		
Italy - ANIOS				X		
Kosovo						X
Latvia	X					
Lithuania					X	
Malta	X					
Netherlands	X					
Norway	X					
Poland	X			X		
Portugal	X			X		
Romania			X	X		
Russia	X			X		
Scotland	X					
Serbia - ATSZJ	X			X		
Serbia - UTLOSS	X					
Slovenia	X					
Spain	X		X			
Sweden	X					
Switzerland – Fr.	X					
Switzerland – Ge.	X					
Switzerland – It.	X					
Ukraine		X		X		

Figure 3.10

COUNTRY	Government / agency	Employer	Deaf club	Deaf person	Other	NA
Fig. 3.11: LEGAL SETTING						
Responsible party for the payment of the interpreting services						
Albania						X
Austria	X			X		
Belgium - Flanders	X					
Belgium - Wallonia	X					
Bosnia-Herzegovina	X					
Croatia	X					
Cyprus	X		X			
Czech Republic	X					
Denmark	X					
England, Wales & NI	X					
Estonia	X	X		X		
Finland	X				X	
France	X			X		
Germany	X			X		
Greece	X	X		X	X	
Hungary	X					
Iceland	X					
Ireland	X			X		
Italy - ANIMU				X		
Italy - ANIOS	X			X		
Kosovo	X					
Latvia	X			X	X	
Lithuania					X	
Malta	X					
Netherlands	X					
Norway	X					
Poland	X			X		
Portugal	X					
Romania	X					
Russia	X	X	X	X		
Scotland	X					
Serbia - ATSZJ	X			X		
Serbia - UTLOSS	X					
Slovenia	X					
Spain	X			X		
Sweden	X					
Switzerland - Fr.	X					
Switzerland - Ge.	X					
Switzerland - It.	X					
Ukraine		X		X		

Figure 3.11

Fig. 3.12: THEATRE SETTING Responsible party for the payment of the interpreting services							
COUNTRY	Government / agency	Employer	Theatre	Deaf club	Deaf person	Other	NA
Albania							X
Austria			X				
Belgium - Flanders	X		X	X	X		
Belgium - Wallonia	X						
Bosnia-Herzegovina						X	
Croatia	X						
Cyprus				X			
Czech Republic		X	X				
Denmark	X						
England, Wales & NI			X				
Estonia	X	X	X		X		
Finland	X		X				
France					X		
Germany			X	X	X	X	
Greece	X				X	X	
Hungary	X						
Iceland			X				
Ireland			X				
Italy - ANIMU					X		
Italy - ANIOS			X	X	X		
Kosovo							X
Latvia						X	
Lithuania						X	
Malta			X			X	
Netherlands	X						
Norway	X		X				
Poland			X		X		
Portugal		X	X				
Romania							X
Russia							X
Scotland			X				
Serbia - ATSZJ							X
Serbia - UTLOSS	X		X			X	
Slovenia						X	
Spain							X
Sweden			X				
Switzerland - Fr.			X	X			
Switzerland - Ge.	X		X				
Switzerland - It.	X						
Ukraine		X	X	X	X		

Figure 3.12

3.10 SIGN LANGUAGE RECOGNITION & FUNDING OF INTERPRETING SERVICES

Figure 3.13 is a combination of the figures 3.5, 3.8, 3.9, 3.10, 3.11 and 3.12. The data indicates the recognition of sign language in a country or region and who is funding the interpreting services in a specific setting (employment, education, medical, legal, theatre). Each country has a different way of funding interpreting services and within a country there are also different possibilities or responsible parties for the payment of the interpreting services.

The overview shows no correlation between the recognition of sign language and the funding of interpreting services. For example, Danish Sign Language is not officially recognized but the government does fund interpreting services in all settings. On the contrary in Kosovo, where sign language was recognized in 2010, there is no funding for interpreting services in employment, medical and theatre settings.

Symbols in figure 3.13

-	No funding provided
G	Government
EM	Employer
E	Educational institution
T	Theatre
DC	Deaf Club
D	Deaf person
O	Other
?	Conflicting data provided by two associations in the same country

COUNTRY	Sign language recognition	Fig. 3.13: Interpreting services funded by				
		Employment	Education	Medical	Legal	Theatre
Albania	No	-	-	-	-	-
Austria	Yes	G	G/E	G	G/D	T
Belgium – Flanders	Yes	G	G	G/D	G	G/T/DC/D
Belgium – Wallonia	Yes	G	G	G	G	G
Bosnia-Herzegovina	Yes	G/EM	G/EM	DC	G	O
Croatia	No	G	G	G	G	G
Cyprus	Yes	DC	G	DC	G/DC	DC
Czech Republic	Yes	G	E	G	G	EM/T
Denmark	No	G	G	G	G	G
England, Wales & NI	Yes	G/EM	G	G	G	T
Estonia	Yes	G/EM	G/EM/E/D	G/EM/D	G/EM/D	G/EM/T/D
Finland	Yes	G/EM	G	G/O	G/O	G/T
France	Yes	EM	G	D	G/D	D
Germany	Yes	G/EM/D	G/E/D	O	G/D	T/DC/D/O
Greece	Yes	G/D/O	G	G/O	G/EM/D/O	D/O
Hungary	Yes	G	G	G	G	G
Iceland	Yes	G	E	G	G	T
Ireland	No	G/EM	G/E	G	G/D	T
Italy	No	D	?	D	?/D	?/D
Kosovo	Yes	-	E	-	G	-
Latvia	Yes	G	G/D	G	G/D/O	O
Lithuania	Yes	O	O	O	O	O
Malta	No	G/EM	G/E	G	G	T/O
Netherlands	No	G	G	G	G	G
Norway	No	G	G	G	G	G/T
Poland	Yes	G/EM/D	E	G/D	G/D	T/D
Portugal	Yes	EM/D	G/D	G/D	G	EM/T
Romania	Yes	EM/DC/D	E/D	DC/D	G	-
Russia	No	G/EM/DC/D	G/E/D	G/D	G/EM/E/D	-
Scotland	Yes	G	G	G	G	T
Serbia	No	?	?	G/?	G/?	?
Slovenia	Yes	EM/O	G	G	G	O
Spain	Yes	G/DC/D	E	DC	G/D	-
Sweden	Yes	G	E	G	G	T
Switzerland – Fr.	Yes	G/E	G	G	G	T/DC
Switzerland – Ge.	No	G	G	G	G	G/T
Switzerland – It.	No	G	G	G	G	G
Ukraine	Yes	EM	EM/E/D	EM/D	EM/D	EM/T/DC/D

Figure 3.13

3.11 INTERPRETING FEES

Fees for freelance work as a sign language interpreter vary per country and region. Not all respondents (Denmark, Estonia, Lithuania, Spain) were able to provide an answer due to how interpreters are employed or paid in their country. The map (figure 3.14) provides a geographical overview of the minimum freelance interpreting fee per hour.

The respondents who provided a range in the fee per hour, the lowest fee was used in both figures (3.14, 3.15). Figure 3.15 provides an overview of the exact numbers.

The survey question contained four sections: interpreting fee per hour and traveling time, traveling expenses, and other expenses (fig. 3.15). The lowest fee per hour is two euros in Albania and the highest fee is 70 euros per hour in the French region of Switzerland. The three highest fees per hour all for all the language regions in Switzerland.

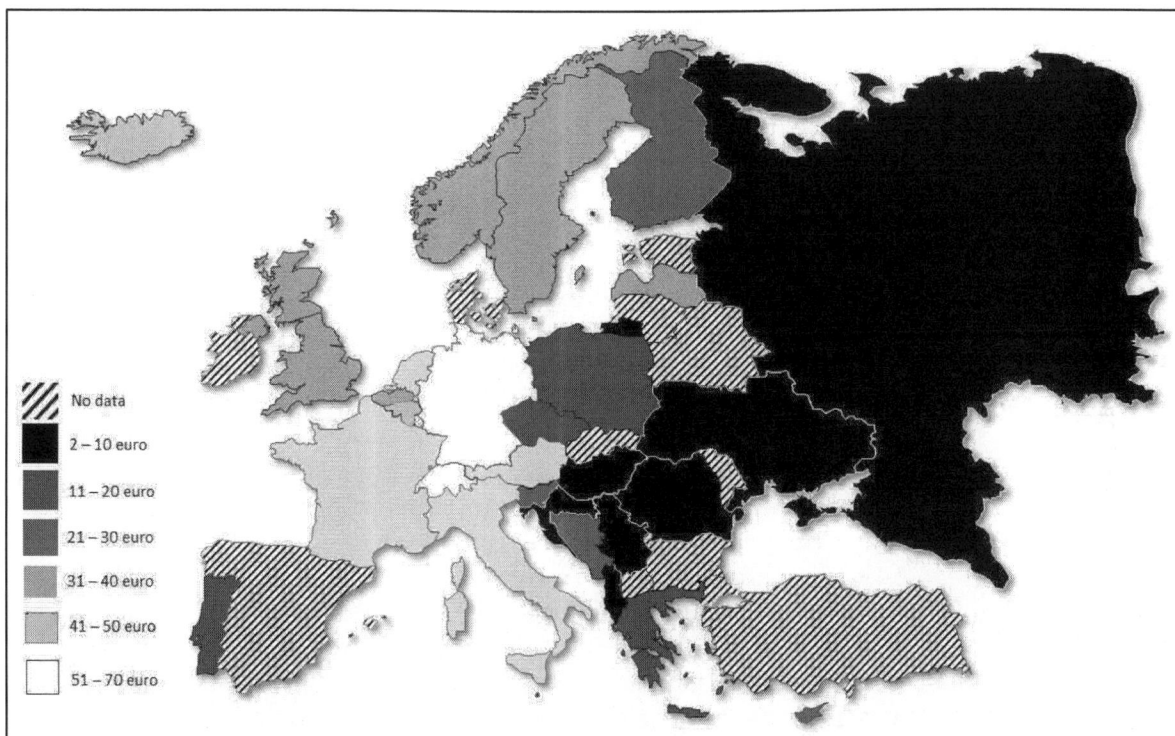

Figure 3.14: Range of minimum fees in euros per hour per country / region

In the majority of the countries the traveling expenses for interpreters are covered, but less often they receive a payment for their traveling time (figure 3.16). Many countries also provide a minimum fee or time per assignment, varying from 15 minutes to three hours. When working in a high level setting or in special settings such as the theatre, legal and conference, some countries provide extra payment. Norway is the only country which mentions extra payment for working for Deafblind persons. In France interpreters also receive extra payment when working on TV and in Spain when working with three languages.

Fig. 3.15: Minimum interpreting fee in euro per freelance hour

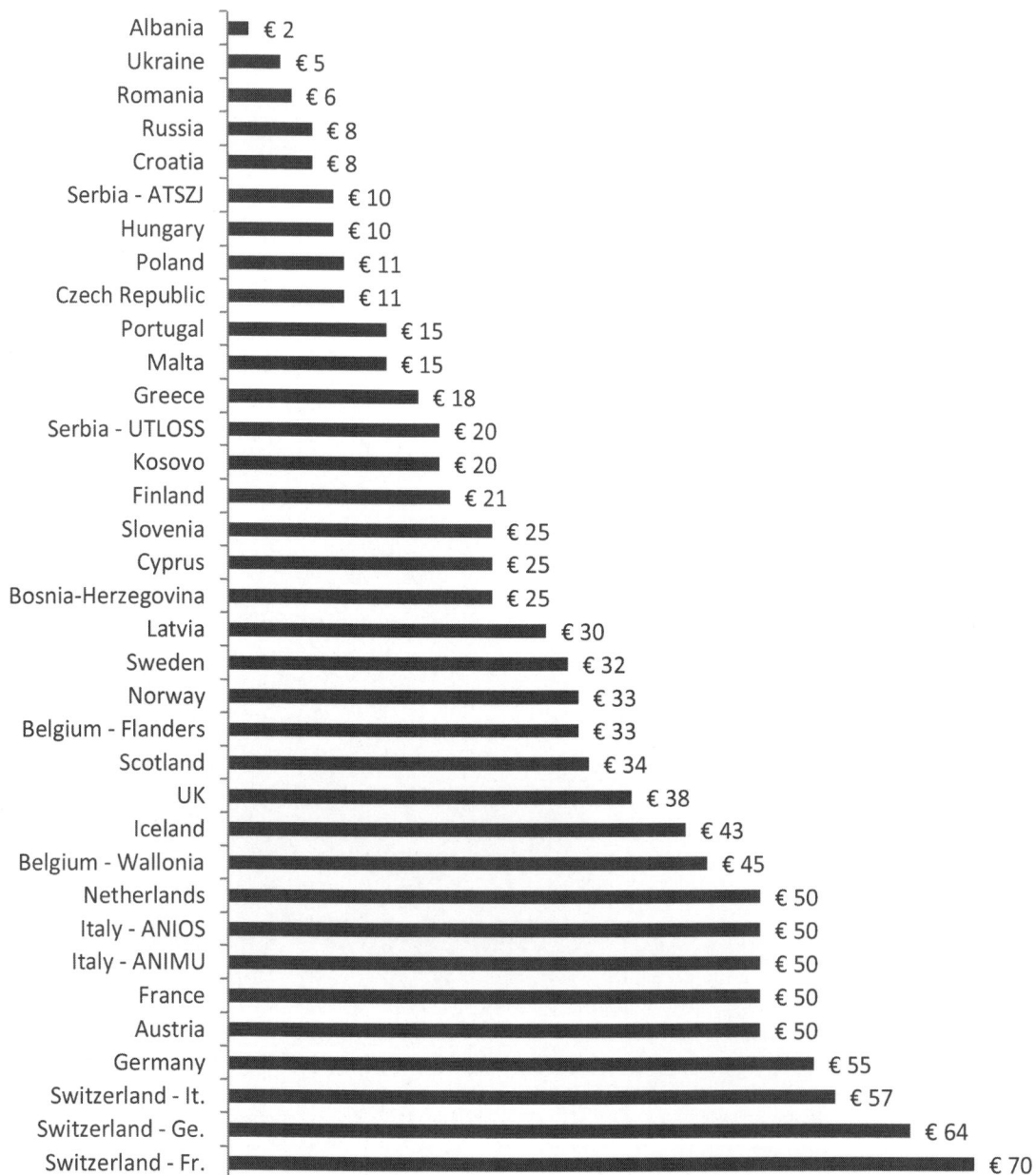

Country	Fee
Albania	€ 2
Ukraine	€ 5
Romania	€ 6
Russia	€ 8
Croatia	€ 8
Serbia - ATSZJ	€ 10
Hungary	€ 10
Poland	€ 11
Czech Republic	€ 11
Portugal	€ 15
Malta	€ 15
Greece	€ 18
Serbia - UTLOSS	€ 20
Kosovo	€ 20
Finland	€ 21
Slovenia	€ 25
Cyprus	€ 25
Bosnia-Herzegovina	€ 25
Latvia	€ 30
Sweden	€ 32
Norway	€ 33
Belgium - Flanders	€ 33
Scotland	€ 34
UK	€ 38
Iceland	€ 43
Belgium - Wallonia	€ 45
Netherlands	€ 50
Italy - ANIOS	€ 50
Italy - ANIMU	€ 50
France	€ 50
Austria	€ 50
Germany	€ 55
Switzerland - It.	€ 57
Switzerland - Ge.	€ 64
Switzerland - Fr.	€ 70

Not included: Denmark, Estonia, Lithuania, Spain

Fig. 3.16: Overview per country of payment for freelance interpreting

Country	Fee per hour	Traveling time	traveling expenses	other	minimum fee or minimum time per assignment?	Extra payment for specialties (e.g. legal, theater, conference interpreting)?
Albania	€ 2	€ 2	€ 2	€ 2	No	No
Austria	€ 50	€ 30	€ 5	0	half an hour	No
Belgium - Flanders	€ 33.41	0	€ 0.25	0.20 per km if the deaf person is paying.	1 hour	theater, conference and politics, sometimes legal settings
Belgium - Wallonia	€ 45-55	0	€ 0.34	0	No	theater, concert (francofolies)
Bosnia-Herzegovina	€ 25	0	0	0	No	No
Croatia	€ 8	0	0	0	No	for legal interpreting
Cyprus	€ 25	0	0	0	€ 25	No
Czech Republic	€ 11	€ 4	included	-	No	conference, theater
Denmark	xxx	xxx	xxx	xxx	1 hour minimum	Legal, theater, conference
Estonia	-	-	-	Most interpreters work for agencies and costs/ conditions differ from locations as well as agencies	Depends on locations and agencies	Depends on the employer
Finland	€ 21.34	€ 7.15	all	-	1 hour	high level €27.49/hour
France	€ 50	-	-	-	No	conference, TV, high classes (universities, seminar)
Germany	€ 55	€ 55	€ 0.30/km	0	No	Depends on negotiations between interpreter and event
Greece	€ 18-20	-	Expenses covered	NO	No	Legal
Hungary	€ 10-12	0	0	0	No	No
Iceland	€ 43 min. rate	negotiable	negotiable		1 hour	est. ave. 30% (both for freelance and the official office)

Country	Fee per hour	Traveling time	traveling expenses	other	minimum fee or minimum time per assignment?	Extra payment for specialties (e.g. legal, theater, conference interpreting)?
Ireland	0	0	tickets	€ 106	3 hours	No
Italy - ANIMU	€ 50	0	Reimbursement	no	1 hour	No
Italy - ANIOS	€ 50					No
Kosovo	€ 20	depends from city	depends on the city	na	2 hours	depends on the events
Latvia	€ 30	0	120	15	€ 7	No
Lithuania	-	-	-	-	No	No
Malta	€ 15-25	NA	NA	NA	1 hour	No
Netherlands	€ 50.35	Incl. in hour fee	€ 0.66 per kilometer	0	30 minutes in private settings, 15 minutes for work and educ.	No
Norway	€ 33.63	€ 20.23	all covered	evenings and weekends: € 42.04	1 hour	interpreting for deafblind, higher rates
Poland	€ 11	0	20	0	No	Conference interpreting is best paid. Sometimes interpreters charge extra fee if their interpreting is to be video-recorded.
Portugal	€ 15.00	0	€ 0.35/km	lunch or dinner	1 hour	conferences and legal
Romania	€ 6	0	bus or train expenses are fully covered. own 7.5 l/ 100 km	subsistence € 3 per day	1 hour	No
Russia	€ 8-12	0 or € 5 per hour	max € 2	varies	hoped for 2 hours in Moscow and € 12, different in regions	court or legal dealing with property
Scotland	€ 34.60	0	€ 18.53	0	€ 69	No
Serbia - ATSZJ	€ 10	0	0	0	Yes	Yes

Country	Fee per hour	Traveling time	traveling expenses	other	minimum fee or minimum time per assignment?	Extra payment for specialties (e.g. legal, theater, conference interpreting)?
Serbia - UTLOSS	€ 20	0	0	0	No	No
Slovenia	€ 25.54	0	€ 0.428	0	until 20 minutes is € 14.19; there is no minimum time (as you start hour)	No
Spain	not relevant	not relevant	not relevant	not relevant	1 hour	working with three languages.
Sweden	€ 32	€ 16	Covered if it is not an outsourced area	we have different rates due to day, evening and weekends and it varies across the country	No	both yes and no, it varies on form of employment, sometimes third language, legal settings.
Switzerland – Fr.	€ 70	€ 30	0	€ 20	€ 70 as an hour even if 30 min	No
Switzerland – Ge.	€ 64	€ 33	see below	0	1 hour	sometimes preparation time
Switzerland – It.	€ 57	€ 26	€ 26	€ 40	€ 57	No
UK	€ 38	0			most freelance charge minimum of 3 hours	depends on the individual and what they negotiate
Ukraine	€ 5-15	NA	NA	NA	No	No

Figure 3.16

CONCLUSION

The sign language interpreter profession has undergone considerable changes since the last publication of 'Sign Language Interpreting in Europe' in 2008. New national associations of sign language interpreters were established and the overall number of working sign language interpreters increased. More countries have developed an independent registration system for sign language interpreters, or are in the process of establishing this.

A significant change are the newly established educational programs for sign language interpreters. In addition, there is a shift from short term to long term and intensive programs, typically leading to a BA degree. The European Forum of Sign Language Interpreters (efsli) explored the educational programs throughout Europe and now provides a platform for the development of a model curriculum to educate sign language interpreters.

A development indirectly related to sign language interpreting, is the legal recognition of a national sign language as a language. In the last years, the majority of the countries within in the European Union have formally undertaken the recognition of sign language. The recognitions are different in status. Some countries have a constitutional recognition, others have recognized sign language in a decree or regulation (Wheatley & Pabsch, 2012). Although one might expect differently, the survey data indicates that the recognition of a sign language does not automatically lead to increased access to interpreting services for Deaf sign language users or to the establishment of interpreter education.

The European Union of the Deaf (EUD) and the European Forum of Sign Language Interpreters (efsli) intensified their collaboration and confirmed this through a working agreement. The EUD and efsli developed guidelines together on how to work with a sign language interpreter and how to provide interpreting services at a European level event.

As a result of the increased attention to Deaf sign language users rights to interpreting services, awareness is on the rise in EU countries. The European parliament and the European Disability Forum have lobbied for freedom of movement for people with a disability. The diversity in the rights and payment of interpreting services in the European countries creates a barrier for Deaf sign language users to work or study abroad (Calle, 2011). The survey data indicates that payment for interpreting services in the Western European countries is available in an increasing number of settings, but can be hindered by the current European financial crisis. In the Eastern part of Europe there are few paid interpreting services available. As a result, sign language interpreters are not able to work professionally

Although the profession has received more recognition during the last five years, sign language interpreters continue to cite their daily struggles to provide equal access to society for Deaf sign language users. By and large, these interpreters are up against the unwillingness and unawareness of the authorities to provide and fund professional interpreting services.

APPENDICES

Note: Appendixes 1 – 4 contain the details of the responses which have not been mentioned in Part 1 – 3.

APPENDIX 1 - ORGANIZATIONS OF SIGN LANGUAGE INTERPRETER IN EUROPE

Country / region	Response on behalf of the association	Name association	Year establishment	Percentage interpreters in country / region as member of association	Other kind of members	Interpreter members in association	Non-interpreter members	Deaf interpreters as members	Annual membership fee interpreter members	Comments
Austria	Yes	Österreichischer Gebärdensprach-DolmetscherInnen-Verband	1998	80%		93	0	No	€ 150,00	
Belgium - Flanders	Yes	BVGT Beroepsvereniging Vlaamse	2009	40%	Students	70	0	No	€ 34,31	Our membership fee follows the payment we get for one hour interpreting. So, last year it was around 33,5 euro.
Belgium - Wallonia	No	ABILS								
Croatia	No	Služba podrške Dodir (Support Service)	1994	I don't know	Students, trainers, volunteers	28	30	Yes	€ 10,00	
Czech Republic	Yes	Czech Chamber of the Sign Language Interpreters	2000	60	Students, Institutes SL researchers, teachers	50	40	Yes	€ 23,20	The number of the members is currently changing as we are counting those who have not paid their membership fee for the year 2012.
Denmark	Yes	Foreningen af Tegnsprogstolke (FTT)	1988	?	Students	250	10	No	€ 66,66	We have members from two different unions (SL and HK) and members from SL get a 10€ discount paid by the union
England, Wales & NI	Yes	Association of Sign Language Interpreters ASLI	1987	?	Students, Institutes Corporate Supporters	639	5	Yes	€ 252,00	

Country / region	Response on behalf of the association	Name association	Year establishment	Percentage interpreters in country / region as member of association	Other kind of members	Interpreter members in association	Non-interpreter members	Deaf interpreters as members	Annual membership fee interpreter members	Comments
Estonia	Yes	Eesti Viipekeele Tõlkide Ühing	1991	76%	Students, Deaf and hearing people, who support the aims and activity of the association	19 + 4 students/unqualified interpreters	3	Yes	€ 10,00	
Finland	Yes	Suomen Viittomakielen Tulkit RY	1982	approx. 83	Students, Institutes, Trainers honorary members	655	144 (student members)	No	1,3 % of ones salary	student member - free institute member/supporting member - 42 €
France	Yes	Association française des interprètes et traducteurs en langue des signes	1978	30	Interpreter agencies	112	0	No	€ 60,00	
Germany	Yes	Bundesverband der GebärdensprachdolmetscherInnen Deutschlands e.V.	1997	?	Students, Trainers	432	34 students	Yes	€ 130,00	in Germany it is not clear how many slis are working there, because the indication "sign language interpreter" is not protected by law. That is why we cannot say which percentage of slis is member in the association.
Greece	Yes	SDENG	1991	95		72	0	No	€ 150,00	

Country / region	Response on behalf of the association	Name association	Year establishment	Percentage interpreters in country / region as member of association	Other kind of members	Interpreter members in association	Non-interpreter members	Deaf interpreters as members	Annual membership fee interpreter members	Comments
Hungary	No	Jelnyelvi Tolmácsok Országos Szövetsége	1994	10-20%	Students, Institutes	we have no actual information	we no actual information	Yes	€ 20,00	
Iceland	Yes	HART Felag Haskolamntaora Taknmalstulka	1998	70%	0	25	0	No	€ 18,50	As of now we have no educated deaf interpreter here in Iceland. All members of our association are educated interpreters.
Ireland	No	Council of Sign Language Interpreters	2011	70	Students associate	50	2	Yes	€ 100,00	CISLI have a lower rate for student interpreter members, and a lower rate for associate members
Italy - ANIMU	Yes	ANIMU	1987	50%	Students, Trainers	120	15	Yes	€ 80,00	
Italy - ANIOS	Yes	ANIOS	1987	50%		95	0	No	€ 130,00	We have the option "support member" but we have no members in this position
Kosovo	Yes	KASLI	2008	90%	Students, Trainers	25	5	No	€ 20,00	
Lithuania	Yes	Lietuvos gestu kalbos verteju asociacija	2009	95%		70	10	Yes	€ 5,80	
Netherlands	Yes	Nederlandse Beroepsvereniging voor Tolken Gebarentaal	1988	85-90%	Students sponsors, newsletter subscriptions	343 (31-12-2011)	182 (31-12-2012, including students)	No	€ 230 (students pay 48,50 both fees not including an automatic membership of PZO, platform for the self-employed = 31,25)	

Country / region	Response on behalf of the association	Name association	Year establishment	Percentage interpreters in country / region as member of association	Other kind of members	Interpreter members in association	Non-interpreter members	Deaf interpreters as members	Annual membership fee interpreter members	Comments
Norway	Yes	Tolkeforbundet	1978	ca. 25 %	Students	111	0	No	€ 91,66	
Poland	Yes	Stowarzyszenie Tłumaczy Polskiego Języka Migowego	2009	About 20%	Students, Trainers	47	7	Yes	€ 11,50	
Portugal	Yes	Associação Nacional e Profissional da Interpretação - Lingua Gestual	2011	20%	Students	42	3	No	€ 24,00	
Romania	Yes	Asociaţia Naţională a Interpreţilor în Limbaj Mimico-Gestual	2008	10%	Students volunteers	4 official interpreters and 10	6	Yes	€ 15,00	
Russia	Yes	региональная общественная организация "Объединения переводчиков жестового языка"	2010	13%	Students, Trainers people who learn RSL	113	8	Yes	€ 24,00	
Scotland	Yes	Scottish Association of Sign Language Interpreters	1981	95%	Students Agencies	80	1	Yes	€ 296,55	
Serbia - ATSZJ	Yes	Asocijacija tumača srpskog znakovnog jezika	2010	20	Students Supporters	31	11	No	€ 4,27	

A Comprehensive Guide to Sign Language Interpreting in Europe, 2012 edition

Country / region	Response on behalf of the association	Name association	Year establish ment	Percentage interpreters in country / region as member of association	Other kind of members	Interpret er members in associati on	Non-inter-preter members	Deaf interpreter s as members	Annual membership fee interpreter members	Comments
Serbia - UTLOSS	Yes	Udruzenje tumaca za lica ostecenoh sluha Srbije	2000	there is no exact data	Students, Institutes	100	50	Yes	€ 10,00	
Slovenia	Yes	Zavod Združenje tolmačev za slovenski znakovni jezik	2004	44		44	0	No	€ 0,00	We associate all interpreters, but have no official membership, that is in the contract of our country basic acts and legislation.
Spain	Yes	FILSE (Federación Española de Intérpretes de Lengua de Signos y Guía-Intérpretes)	2000	10%	Students	500	0	No	€ 50,00	The figure given for the annual membership fee is the average, as each regional association sets its own fee. For their affiliation to FILSE, the associations pay 15€ to FILSE for each of their members. The % of SLIs who are members is based on the total number of qualified SLIs (5000+), not the number of working SLIs, which is much lower.
Sweden	Yes	Sveriges teckenspråktolkars förening	1969	we don't have the statistics	Students, Trainers, Organizations	146	8 honoree members , 6 organizat ions/ agencies, 36 supportiv e members	No	€ 42,00	We have just recently opened up for deaf-interpreters but we demand that they are educated and there is not really an education for them.
Switzerland - French	Yes	ARILS	1996	97%	Former interpreters	35	2	No	€ 150,00	

Country / region	Response on behalf of the association	Name association	Year establishment	Percentage interpreters in country / region as member of association	Other kind of members	Interpreter members in association	Non-interpreter members	Deaf interpreters as members	Annual membership fee interpreter members	Comments
region										
Switzerland - German region	Yes	Berufsvereinigung der Gebärdensprachdol metscher bgd	1991	99	Students	52	9	No	€ 312,00	
Switzerland - Italian region	Yes	ILISSI	2001	80%	Speech therapist	8	1	No	€ 42,00	In Switzerland there is not one national association, each linguistic region has its association

A Comprehensive Guide to Sign Language Interpreting in Europe, 2012 edition

APPENDIX 2 - REGISTRY OF INTERPRETERS

Country / region	Official name of registry	Number of sign language interpreters registered in the registration	website	Registration body part of your national association of sign language interpreters	Registration body part of another association	Prerequisites to be in the registry as a sign language interpreter	Comments
Austria	Berufseignungsprüfung	95		Yes	No	commissional exam	
Belgium - Flanders	VAPH Vlaams Agentschap voor Personen met een Handicap	?	vaph.be	No	No	You have to sign a form and give a copy of your diploma.	It is not really a "registration body" as we know from the Netherlands, it is the government that registers all the people who wants to interpret. But there are no further consequences.
Belgium - Wallonia	registre de la plate-forme Christian François	12		Yes	No	First of all, the interpreters have to follow a continued training secondly, they have to accept to answer to any kind of complaint	
Cyprus	ΟΜΟΣΠΟΝΔΙΑ ΚΩΦΩΝ ΚΥΠΡΟΥ (CYPRUS DEAF FEDERATION)	15		No	No	To receive permission from Deaf Federation's Board and to attend a seminar through Ministry of Education and Culture (which is not active yet).	
Czech Republic	Centrum zprostředkování tlumočníků pro neslyšící	41	http://www.asnep.cz/tlumoceni/databaze.htm	No	Yes	The interpreter has to pass an entrance exam. But currently as there is lack of the interpreters the organization is going to let the interpreters who do not pass the exam register as well, but they will have to pass the exam in two years period. The interpreters in the registry have to prove their education as well - 150 hours.	This registry is not led by the Czech government. It is administered by an umbrella organization ASNEP. As ASNEP is one of the SL interpreting services providers, it is not independent. The goal of the Czech interpreters is to create an independent body - registry.

70

Country / region	Official name of registry	Number of sign language interpreters registered in the registration	website	Registration body part of your national association of sign language interpreters	Registratio n body part of another association	Prerequisites to be in the registry as a sign language interpreter	Comments
England, Wales & NI	the National Register of Communication Professionals working with Deaf and Deafblind People	737 sign language interpreters & 237 trainee sign language interpreters (source: NCRPD)	www.nrcpd.org.uk	No	No	To have passed the relevant qualification for the category you are applying for	
Estonia	SA Kutsekoda	25	http://kutsekoda.ee/et/index	No	No	The candidate must pass a qualification exam and obtain a qualification certificate.	
Finland	tulkkirekisteri	all graduated interpreters (approx. 750-800)	-	No	No	an exam consisting of interpreting both signing and voicing + self-assessment	So far there is no official, nationwide interpreter certification system. Upon graduation trained interpreters join an informal register maintained jointly by non-profit organizations. Once a person is in the register, she/he is free to work as an interpreter. This current register is not officially monitored by anyone and there no account is taken of individual interpreters' skills and work experience
Hungary	Jelnyelvi Tolmácsok Országos Névjegyzéke	approx. 40	www.nrszh.hu	No	No	-certificate of good conduct (criminal record check) - sign language interpreter education certificate - 300hours interpreting practicing in the last 3years - paying the registration fee	The registration body belongs to the National Office for Rehabilitation and Social Affairs, it is a formal body which maintains the list of interpreters. Registration just has recently begun, so about 40 interpr. will be on the list in the near future.
Ireland	SLIS	41					

A Comprehensive Guide to Sign Language Interpreting in Europe, 2012 edition

Country / region	Official name of registry	Number of sign language interpreters registered in the registration	website	Registration body part of your national association of sign language interpreters	Registration body part of another association	Prerequisites to be in the registry as a sign language interpreter	Comments
Netherlands	Stichting RTG	400	www.stichtingrtg.nl	No	No	-You must have a Bachelor degree certificate of 'Dutch Sign Language Interpreter' by Hogeschool Utrecht OR/AND -You must have a foreign certificate of 'Sign Language Interpreter' and be registered in a foreign 'Registry of Sign Language Interpreters -Obey to the code of ethics -Obtain 60 CEU's in 4 years	
Poland	Rejestr tłumaczy polskiego języka migowego, systemu językowo-migowego i sposobu komunikowania się osób głuchoniewidomych	It is not yet known, because the register has just been introduced.	The registers are run by particular provinces (16).	No	No	The person who wants to be registered as an interpreter needs to submit application forms to the respective office. In the application forms the person declares his/her knowledge of either Polish Sign Language, signed Polish (sign supported Polish) or methods of communication for the Deaf-blind. If in possession, the person may submit certificates or any other documents confirming that fact.	
Romania	Direcția Generală Protecția Persoanelor cu Handicap	52	http://www.anph.ro	No	No	the diploma in sign language courses, high school diploma, record, medical certificate, copy of identity card, copy of birth certificate and copy of marriage certificate (if you are married).	Even though there are 52 sign language interpreters, only 26 are interpreting.
Scotland	Scottish Association of Sign Language	80	www.sasli.co.uk	Yes	No	NVQ6 or Equivilant	
Slovenia	Ministrstvo za delo, družino insocialne zadeve	44	www.mddsz.gov.si	No	No	date of entry in register, name and surname of interpreter, date and number of getting the certificate	Ministry, which leads the registry, is governmental body.
Switzerland - Italian region	Procom	8	www.procom-deaf.ch	No	Yes		

APPENDIX 3 – RIGHT TO AN INTERPRETER

Country or region	Does a Deaf person have a right to an interpreter in your country / region?	What do these rights to an interpreter consist of?	Internet link to the legal text of the interpreting law	Comments
Albania	No			
Austria	Partly	service at job partly at private settings partly in school at university		
Belgium - Flanders	Yes	For each year they get several different kinds of hours paid by the government. For ex: 10% off their working time the government will pay the interpreter.	http://www.cabvlaanderen.be/doc /Deontologische%20Code%20nieu w%202009.pdf	We are working on a new code for interpreting. Witch can result in some new laws.
Belgium - Wallonia	Partly	Deaf person has right to an interpreter but there are not enough interpreters to answer all requests.		
Bosnia-Herzegovina	Yes	Interpreters codec that we have right now		
Croatia	Partly	There is one law on Social welfare which mentions the right to an interpreter, however it is only a right on paper		
Cyprus	Yes	Their rights consist of approximately 6 times per year for 2 hours maximum each time to be covered by the Cyprus Deaf Federation and as a prerequisite the deaf person needs to be a member of the Cyprus Deaf Federation.	Not applicable yet.	
Czech Republic	Yes	Right to choose the means of communication according to the person´s preferences. Right to have an education in person´s preferred language.	http://ruce.cz/clanky/506-zakon-o-komunikacnich-systemech-neslysicich-a-hluchoslepych-osob	2008: amendment to the Act of communication systems of deaf and Deafblind people
Denmark	Yes	You have the right to an interpreter in almost every situation. Education, legal settings, work related, private matters ex. weddings, funerals, attending courses and so on.		
England, Wales & NI	Yes	The Equality Act 2010 states that service providers and retailers have to ensure equality of access for all disabled people with reasonable adjustment. The last part of the sentence is important as some service providers use that as an excuse to preclude SL provision due to cost. however medical and legal provision must be catered for.	http://www.legislation.gov.uk/ukpg a/2010/15/contents	
Estonia	Yes	The communication of a deaf or hard of hearing person (SL or signed spoken language users) in personal errands is made available by interpreting services.	https://www.riigiteataja.ee/akt/11 8032011001 § 8. (2)	
Finland	Yes	Interpretation services comprise all interpretation in sign language to manage work, study, everyday affairs, social participation, leisure activities, recreation or any other corresponding purpose. Educational interpreting - unlimited leisure, work, family etc. - minimum 180h /year for deaf, 360h / year for Deafblind. More interpreting hours when applying	This is provided only in Finnish: http://www.finlex.fi/fi/laki/kokoel ma/2010/20100025.pdf	
France	Yes	Deaf people have the right to ask for an interpreter but he has to pay....	No legal text...	

A Comprehensive Guide to Sign Language Interpreting in Europe, 2012 edition

Country or region	Does a Deaf person have a right to an interpreter in your country / region?	What do these rights to an interpreter consist of?	Internet link to the legal text of the interpreting law	Comments
Germany	Partly	Communicate in German sign language if needed according to medical settings, governmental acts, and legal settings. Costs are paid by law or health insurances and court.		No federal law. Every federal state has its own regulations. Official recognition only in social law „Sozialgesetzbuch"
Greece	Yes	The deaf person has to be registered in one of the deaf clubs which are members of the deaf federation.	No	
Hungary	Yes	Sign language law gives the right to use interpreting several part of the life. 120hours/year/person is state-funded, +120hours/year for students. Total 36.000hours/year interpretation of public service free.	Act CXXV of 2009 on Hungarian Sign Language and the use of Hungarian Sign Language: www.sinosz.hu/english version	The law was born, but harmonization, and implementing regulation is very slow and difficult.
Iceland	Yes	Authorities in Iceland, Governmental and local are by law (passed in May 2011) to ensure that: "All those who need service in Icelandic Sign Language are guaranteed that right of service. "Laws nr. 61 passed June 2011, Art. 13.	Laws regarding the status of the Icelandic language and Icelandic Sign Language Law nr. 61/2011 (in Icelandic). Http://www.althingi.is/altext/139/s/pdf/1570.pdf	
Ireland	No			They have a right to reasonable accommodation
Italy - ANIMU	No			
Italy - ANIOS	Partly	In some legal setting the deaf person has the right to an interpreter. There is a Law (104/92) which states in article 9 "The municipalities can provide the deaf person with sign language interpreting if they have no money on their balance". As a result in 20 years few cities have followed this article of the law.		We are fighting strongly in the Italian parliament to receive the recognition of LIS. In Italy there is a strong lobby of doctors and the industries on cochlear implants, so it is hard to achieve a law to recognize LIS. The Deaf people have severe difficulties in accessing some basic services like health or public administration.
Kosovo	Yes	Now the Government of Kosovo together with the Kosovar Association of the Deaf and Kosovo Association of Sign Language Interpreters are working on the national program to offer the sign language service for Deaf people which means on establishing the unit for sign language interpreting service.		
Latvia	Yes	The interpreter is provided at the national level to tackle social issues, and vocational and higher education	Ministru kabineta noteikumi Nr.291 Rīgā 2003.gada 3.jūnijā (prot. Nr.32 31.§) Prasības sociālo pakalpojumu sniedzējiem	
Lithuania	Yes	-		
Malta	No			
Netherlands	Yes	30 hours for private settings (168 for the Deafblind). 15% of total working-hours in work related settings 100% of the time scheduled for a study in hearing education also in legal settings	www.overheid.nl – staatscourrant – seach for 'beleidsregels intermediaire activiteiten'	Government provides funding for the service however it is not a legal right yet.
Norway	Yes	Right to have an interpreter in any situation, f.ex. Work, education, daily life. Daily life could be a family dinner with non-SL speaking relatives, weddings, evening courses,	Daily life, work, health and education: Forvaltningsloven	

Country or region	Does a Deaf person have a right to an interpreter in your country / region?	What do these rights to an interpreter consist of?	Internet link to the legal text of the interpreting law	Comments
		mountain hiking with guide etc. There are no charges for the deaf, the state provides the interpreter.	chapter 10, § 10 : http://www.lovdata.no/all/tl-19970228-019-034.html#10-1 Legalsettings: Domstolloven § 137: http://www.lovdata.no/all/tl-19150813-005-009.html#137	
Poland	Yes	Deaf people may use interpreting services in institutions and offices understood as public administration, healthcare, emergency services. They have to inform the institution about their need to use an interpreter at least 3 days before the planned appointment. The interpreter is chosen from a special register according to communication preferences of the Deaf person.	http://www.niepelnosprawni.gov.pl/aktualnosci/archiwum-aktualnosci/go:1/art160.html	
Portugal	Yes	Deaf people have to pay an interpreter to go to the bank, doctor, etc.	http://arquivo.ese.ips.pt/ese/cursos/Lei_89-99.pdf	In 1997 our sign language was recognized as official language but only in education: deaf people have the right to access to knowledge in their own language (but only in special schools). To overcome, schools have sign language interpreters.
Romania	Partly	The law says that the deaf person has the right to an interpreter when there are cases that handle with police, court/justice, and banks. For other issues (like hospital) the deaf person has the right to an interpreter but he needs to pay for this services.	http://legeaz.net/legea-448-2006/	
Russia	Partly	Depends on the region of the country, usually 40 hours of free interpreting per year per Deaf person	"Individual rehabilitation program of the person with disabilities"	Hopefully many things will change soon due to lobbying campaign of the RASLI, Russian Deaf Organization, Centre for Deaf Studies and the ratification of the UN Convention
Scotland	Yes	Access to Health Appointments Access to Education Access to Theatre Access to Police/Court/Legal Settings Access to Employment Access to Social Services	N/A	British Sign Language was officially recognized in the United Kingdom in 2003. It was officially recognized by Scottish Government in March 2011

A Comprehensive Guide to Sign Language Interpreting in Europe, 2012 edition

Country or region	Does a Deaf person have a right to an interpreter in your country / region?	What do these rights to an interpreter consist of?	Internet link to the legal text of the interpreting law	Comments
Serbia - ATSZJ	Partly	Ministry of Labor and Social policy from 2010 finance apx. 200 euro per month local Deaf organization to provide interpreting service to Deaf local community. Deaf person have right to use (bring) interpreter at all settings except court as long as those institution don't have obligation to pay for service. There are 9 registered interpreters in Court, registered 1997, in entire Serbia and only they can interpret in Court. Most Deaf people cannot afford them because their services are too expensive. Court pays interpreter services only in Criminal Proceedings.	Interpreters and sign language are mentioned in following laws: Constitution of the Republic of Serbia Article 32 http://www.srbija.gov.rs/cinjenice_o_srbiji/ustav_odredbe.php?id=218 Law on Higher Education of the Republic of Serbia Article 80 http://www.doktoranti.org/documents/Zakon%20o%20visokom%20obrazovanju. pdf Health Protection Law Article 28 http://www.zdravlje.gov.rs/tmpmz-admin/downloads/zakoni1/zakon_zdravstvena_zastita.pdf Law on the Prohibition of Discrimination http://www.ilo.org/wcmsp5/groups/public/---ed_protect/---protrav/---ilo_aids/documents/legaldocument/wcms_128034.pdf Law on Prevention of Discrimination against Persons with Disabilities http://www.paragraf.rs/propisi/zakon_o_sprecavanju_diskriminacije_osoba_sa_i nvaliditetom.html	Republic of Serbia ratified UN CRPD in 2009.In 2010 the Ministry of Labor and Social policy formed the working group that would prepare the draft of the Law on Serbian Sign Language. So far we don't have any information regarding draft law.
Serbia - UTLOSS	No			
Slovenia	Yes	- the right to SLI in every state or local body, every public institution - the right to 30 hours (as vouchers) for personal business (and students 100 hours)	www.tolmaci.si	
Spain	Yes	The law recognizing sign language talks of giving sign language users access to Education, Training and Employment, Healthcare, Culture, Sport and Leisure, Transport, Public Administration, Media and Information. In all cases explicit mention of interpreting services is given. There are no specific provisions and unfortunately the provision set out in the law has not materialized in the five years since it was passed.	http://www.boe.es/boe/dias/2007/10/24/pdfs/A43251-43259.pdf	
Sweden	Partly	www.sdr.org	www.sdr.org	
Switzerland - French region	Yes	According to different handicap laws the right is full during school and professional studies and it's free for the deaf person and institute. The right is a fee of max 1'580 CHF/month for professional interviews or settings... Interpreters are free for private needs and a global fee is asked for deaf clubs, institutes for the deaf...(about chf100/half day) but a high fee is asked to official and public services (chf 150/hour) : Legal, hospital..		
Switzerland - German region	Yes	- a certain amount of interpr. hours for private use - a certain amount of interpr. hours for work - interpreting hours for each education or further education has to be approved by the government first - interpreting hours for official departments have to be paid directly from these departments		
Switzerland - Italian region	Partly	Private requests of those entitled to AI Private requests by persons entitled to AI are free for the following offices up to 23.00: workplace, if there is a decision AI or AI has been applied courses and further training if there is a decision under Art AI. 16 (apply 2-3 months before the question whether AI is yet to be forwarded) school (parent meeting), to communicate the school's address so that PROCOM can submit the invoice to the school interviews with agencies and public offices (labor office,	http://www.procom-deaf.ch/it/Tarife.aspx	

Country or region	Does a Deaf person have a right to an interpreter in your country / region?	What do these rights to an interpreter consist of?	Internet link to the legal text of the interpreting law	Comments
		tax office, social security office, registry office, the office runs and failures) communicate the address of the office concerned so that PROCOM can submit the same invoice at the office medical assignments for private (weddings, anniversaries, family celebrations) classes (present time the request), free time		
Ukraine	Yes	Government agencies and organizations of local self-government facilitate the provision of sign language interpreting services for the hearing impaired citizens of Ukraine who use the sign language.	http://zakon 1.rada.gov.u a/laws/show /875-12	The main function of providing sign language interpreters services is the Ukrainian Society of the Deaf. The Law "On Amending Certain Laws of Ukraine on the Rights of Persons with Disabilities" (upd Dec 22, 2011): "Article 23. Sign language as the language of hearing impaired is the means of communication and education and is protected by the state. Government agencies and organs of local self-government • contribute to the dissemination of sign language and the promotion of the linguistic identity of hearing impaired; • ensure the preservation, study and full development of sign language, using it as a means of education, training, teaching, communication and creative process; • provide the possibility of communication for the hearing impaired in the government bodies, facilities and social protection institutions, law-enforcement authorities, fire safety facilities, emergency rescue teams, health care institutions, educational organizations, etc.; • facilitate the provision of sign language interpreting services for the hearing impaired citizens of Ukraine who use the sign language; • create conditions for the scientific research of the sign language; • promote the use of sign language in official relations. Broadcasters (regardless of ownership and departmental subordination) provide subtitling or sign language interpretation of official announcements, movies, videos, broadcasts and TV programs on terms and conditions specified by the Cabinet of Ministers of Ukraine."

APPENDIX 4 - EMPLOYMENT

Country / region	Working interpreters	Sufficient number of interpreters	... because:	Does an interpreter earn reasonable payment for the work he or she does?	... because:	Comments
Albania	6	No	there only 6 sign language interpreters	No	there is no low to ensure employment policy for this new profession	
Austria	120	No	often no service possible	No	partly yes partly have to fight for, and not enough	
Belgium - Flanders	160	No	most people have another job as well	No	it less than a person who's jobless and get government support	
Belgium - Wallonia	12	No	there is no educational program to become sign interpreter and a part of interpreters work part time	No	she is not paid for preparation	
Bosnia-Herzegovina	none	No	no one pays them	No		Payment of the interpreters in our country is regulated with the law, but same law is not being respected in global. Often comes the situation that the deaf person pays for their own costs of interpreting besides the law on the use of sign language
Croatia	10 are active interpreters	No		No		We have interpreters working for our Support Services but they are not employed since the government does not offer financing for full time employment. All interpreters who are working for the agency have other full time jobs and interpret in their free time
Cyprus	15	No	Most of the times interpreters work at other sites (personal job) and they are not available for interpretation.	I do not know	From the Federation are paid a reasonable amount, from other settings no.	Interpreters regularly are paid 25euros per hour under the Cyprus Deaf Federation and Deaf Clubs. For legal settings when paid by the government they receive around 15-20 euros (with no travelling included).

Country / region	Working interpreters	Sufficient number of interpreters	... because:	Does an interpreter earn reasonable payment for the work he or she does?	... because:	Comments
Denmark	We don't know the exact number but approx. 300-350	I do not know		Yes		
England, Wales & NI	700+	I do not know		Yes	the average hourly charge is ok	
Estonia	25 qualified interpreters, but there are also some unqualified "interpreters" working (no exact number known)	No	Depends on the location - bigger cities have more interpreters to meet more effectively the needs of the clients	No	Most interpreters need a full time job other than interpreting for making a living	
Finland	600-700	I do not know		No	interpreters salary is not near the average salary for other high educated professionals in Finland	"Freelance interpreters" payment for hours is what hourly based working interpreters are earning. They are not usually full time working. Most interpreters are monthly paid, and are earning approx. 2400€ /month (gross wage)
France	360	No	Around 100 000 signers... 360 interpreters aren't enough...	No	Generally no but the colleagues who only work on conference or TV... OK	It's difficult to answer to this question: "How much does a freelance interpreter (on average) earn (in euros)?" because it depends of the situation (legal setting, educational setting, conference...), of the location (Paris, country...), of the statute. (freelancer, employee...).
Germany	No number can be provided. Not every interpreter is registered. Profession is not protected by law so that there is no sure number how many people work as sli in Germany.	No	Interpreter education programs are young. Only few students enroll every year, not every student graduates or works as interpreter after studies. Right to use sl is young, too. Little Information about the right to use an interpreter. Deaf people now more and more recognize that they can use interpreters and start using more interpreters. Young Deaf people striving for better education in which more interpreters are needed.	No	Not in every setting. Preparation time is not paid. For every setting same fee is paid, no matter how demanding it is or how much time the interpreter needs in advance for preparation.	

A Comprehensive Guide to Sign Language Interpreting in Europe, 2012 edition

Country / region	Working interpreters	Sufficient number of interpreters	... because:	Does an interpreter earn reasonable payment for the work he or she does?	... because:	Comments
Hungary	70-90	No	In education need more.	No	it is monthly aprx.400-500eur is enough only for life minimum	In Hungary the sign language interpreting is not so respected, and also not financed well. The professional recognition only on paper, the social acceptance is big challenge for the interpreters in Hungary.
Iceland	27	I do not know	opinion varies in group of interpreters			
Ireland	60	No	unbalanced seasonal demand (education work)	I do not know	seasonal & regional factors	Due to the effects of the economic recession coupled with the stage of development of the profession in terms of national data, national register, etc. we are unable to answer this question well.
Italy - ANIMU	200	I do not know		Yes	it's ok	
Italy - ANIOS	100	Yes	All the service is paid by the deaf persons themselves. The Deaf persons book the professional interpreters only in some important meetings, and not in other settings.	No	we have to pay 50% to taxes	
Kosovo	12	No		No	because spoken interpreters earn more	
Latvia	20	Yes		I do not know		
Lithuania	100	I do not know		I do not know		
Malta	3 full time & 4 freelance	No	only 3 full time and freelance have other full time jobs and work only occasionally	No	The work involves a professional commitment and responsibility and is estimated to be less paid than for other professional work	

Country / region	Working interpreters	Sufficient number of interpreters	... because:	Does an interpreter earn reasonable payment for the work he or she does?	... because:	Comments
Netherlands	about 400	I do not know		Yes	The fee in itself is reasonable, but some improvement could be made in paying different fees for different skills. Now, all interpreters are paid equally in all possible settings	Are there sufficient interpreters to meet the requests? It depends on how you look at it. We hear some colleagues find there are too many interpreters in the field, but when (fairly paid) team interpreting were possible as it used to be (two interpreters for an assignment lasting longer than two hours) there wouldn't be enough interpreters to meet the requests...
Norway	approx. 500	No	the demand isn't covered	No	I'll comment in next section	For those who work for the government the wages are still low for a person who has a BA. For the freelancers the hourly rates are quite good, but we don't have the same welfare systems as the employed. F.ex. we have to cover 16 sick days ourselves and have our own retirement saving program.
Poland	About 200	No	Sometimes it is difficult to make an appointment at a short notice, there are shortages of academic interpreters, there are no interpreters specialized in particular domains.	No	Interpreters are not able to make a living out of interpreting only.	
Portugal - I	65	Yes	are few requests but if there are many the interprets are enough	No	There is a lot of effort in some specialties and it is earn unreasonable	
Portugal - II	+/- 100	No	In some schools interpreters aren't enough and some subjects are left behind.	No	Interpreters in Portugal do any kind of specialty counting on their capacities and never had special training in different areas.	About the question "Is there a minimum fee or minimum time per assignment?", it depends on the interpreter; sometimes interpreters charge a minimum of one hour.
Romania	33	No	the society are not aware of the existence of deaf people	No	the act of parliament decided the fee/interpreting hour and this was decided in 2006	

A Comprehensive Guide to Sign Language Interpreting in Europe, 2012 edition

Country / region	Working interpreters	Sufficient number of interpreters	... because:	Does an interpreter earn reasonable payment for the work he or she does?	... because:	Comments
Scotland	80	No	Of Limited Access to funding for Interpreter Training Programs	I do not know	No Increase in fees for 5 years. Cost of living/inflation and fuel have increased steadily throughout the years	Until 2011 SASLI established recommended Guidelines for Fees, However in 2011 SASLI had to withdraw Recommended Guidelines for Fees due to legal implications. Interpreters charge per mile for travel, no travel time is charged Interpreters can now charge what they wish, however it is my belief that many interpreters remain within the old recommended guidelines.
Serbia - ATSZJ	~ 50	No	There are no professional interpreters in Serbia who can meet the needs of Deaf people in all settings, especially in higher education– education overall, medical settings- especially mental health, Court, police etc.	No		Ministry of Labor and Social policy pays 150 euro for interpreter service per month, regardless if it is Belgrade with 5000 persons or small town with 20 Deaf persons. Court interpreters official fee is 12 euro per hour, but interpreters don't get less than 50 -100 euro for a hearing(appear), from Court and if the party is paying. Conference interpreting - minimum two hours 50 euro or 100 euro per day (interpreters are engaged very rarely- apx. twice a year). Media interpreting -11 euros per 5 minutes live broadcasting news.
Serbia - UTLOSS	no data	I do not know		No	poorly paid	
Slovenia	44	No	Mostly centered in Ljubljana (center of Slovenia)	Yes		
Spain	667	No	There are not enough jobs or financial resources.	No	The profession is not properly valued and the contracting/management of public funds is in the hands of organizations that want to try to do as much as possible with as little as possible.	Much interpreting is paid with public funding given to and administered by Deaf People's Associations. There are no set rules or fees for hiring interpreters. Freelance interpreters do not really exist and most SLIs are on contract: the average full-time monthly salary is probably less than 1000€ (which works out at about 12.5€/hour if they interpret 20 hours a week).
Sweden	we don't know there is no statistics	I do not know		No		For the question: Are there sufficient interpreters to meet the requests? Money rules so both yes and no.

Country / region	Working interpreters	Sufficient number of interpreters	... because:	Does an interpreter earn reasonable payment for the work he or she does?	... because:	Comments
Switzerland – Ge. region	52	Yes	Very low percentage of interpr. cancellations	Yes		
Switzerland – It. region	7	Yes	the request are not so much	Yes		
Ukraine	350	No	One interpreter for 500 deaf sign language users	No	in comments	Freelance interpreters do not really exist and most SLIs are on contract: the average full-time monthly salary is around 1200€. This works out at about 8.5€/hour, or 15€/hour if the workload is 20 hours interpreting a week (and the interpreter will probably be assigned other duties for the remaining 15 hours a week). From a recent (2011) survey of members we know that 82% of SLIs have a temporary contract, 16% have a permanent contract and 2% are freelance.

APPENDIX 5 - SURVEY SIGN LANGUAGE INTERPRETING IN EUROPE

Sign Language Interpreting in Europe - 2012

Your contact details
Please fill out your name and email address. I can then contact you if I need a clarification on your answers.
-   First name *
-   Last name *
-   Email address *

-   Your country / region
-   Which country or region are you reporting on? *
-   Does your country have a national association for sign language interpreters? *

National Association of Sign Language Interpreters
-   Are you reporting on behalf of your association? yes/no
-   What is the official name of your association (in the original language)?
-   What is the email address of your association?
-   What is the web address of your association?
-   In which year was your association officially established?
-   What percentage of interpreters in your country / region is a member of your association?
-   Does your association have other members, beside interpreter members, in their association (tick all that apply)?
    -   Students
    -   Institutes
    -   Trainers
    -   Other, namely
-   How many interpreter members does your association have?
-   How many non-interpreter members does your association have?
-   Does your association have Deaf interpreters as members? yes/no
-   What is the annual membership fee for an interpreter member (in euros)?
    If your membership fee is not in euro, please go here to the currency converter:
    http://www.oanda.com/currency/converter/
-   If you have any comments on this topic, please note them here:

Registration body
-   Is there an official registration body for sign language interpreters in your country / region? yes/no
-   How many sign language interpreters are registered in the registration body?
-   What is the official name of the registry (in your language)?
-   If the registration body has a website, please fill out the web address here:
-   Is the registration body part of your national association of sign language interpreters? yes/no
-   Is the registration body part of another association? yes/no
-   What are the prerequisites to be in the registry as a sign language interpreter?
-   If you have any comments on this topic, please note them here:

Education & Training
-   Does your country / region have an educational program for sign language interpreters? yes/no
-   How many formal educational programs are there in your country or region? *
-   Program(s): Fill out the details of the program

- Name
- City
- Number of years?
- Part or full time?
- Total number of students enrolled?
- Level (Vocational, BA, MA)
- Approximately how many currently working interpreters in your country / region graduated from an interpreter training program?
- How many students have graduated in total (since the start) of the interpreting program?
- If you have any comments on this topic, please note them here:

Right to an interpreter
- Approximately how many Deaf sign language users are there in your country / region?
- Is sign language formally recognized in your country / region? yes/no
- In which year was sign language officially recognized?
- Does a Deaf person have a right to an interpreter in your country / region? yes/no/partly
- What do these rights to an interpreter consist of?
- If you have an internet link to the legal text of the interpreting law in your country, please provide it here:
- If you have any comments on this topic, please note them here:

Employment
- How many interpreters are currently working in your country / region?
- Are there sufficient interpreters to meet the requests?
- How do interpreters work in your country / region?
    - All as freelancers
    - All for an agency
    - Some as freelancers, some for an agency
    - Mostly as freelancers, some for an agency
    - Mostly for an agency, some as freelancers
    - Other, namely
- Who is responsible for the payment of the interpreter in the following situations? Tick all that apply per setting (work, education, medical, legal, theatre):
    - Government / agency
    - Employer
    - Educational program
    - Theatre
    - Deaf club
    - Deaf person Other
    - NA
- How much does a freelance interpreter (on average) earn (in euros)?
    - per interpreting hour
    - for traveling time
    - for traveling expenses
    - other
- Is there a minimum fee or minimum time per assignment?
- Does an interpreter receive extra payment for specialties (e.g. legal, theater, conference
- interpreting)?
- Does an interpreter earn reasonable payment for the work he or she does?
- If you have any comments on this topic, please note them here:

Thank you for participating in the survey!

APPENDIX 6 - OVERVIEW OF FACTS BY COUNTRY

Albania

Population:	3,215,988
Area:	28,748 sq km
Spoken language:	Tosk Albanian
Sign language:	Albanian Sign Language
Sign language recognized:	No
Deaf sign language Users:	1000
Interpreters currently working:	6
Interpreter training program:	0
Interpreter organization:	no

Austria

Population:	8,419,00
Area:	83,858 sq km
Spoken language:	German, Slovenian, Croatian
Sign language:	Austrian Sign Language
Sign language recognized:	2005
Deaf sign language Users:	10,000
Interpreters currently working:	120
Interpreter training program:	3
Interpreter organization:	österreichischer Gebärdensprach DolmetscherInnen-Verband (OEGSDV) e-mail: info@oegsdv.at web site: www.oegsdv.at

Belgium – Flanders & Wallonia

Population:	11,008,00
Area:	30,510 sq km
Spoken languages:	Flemish, French, German
Sign language:	Flemish Sign Language, French Belgian Sign Language
Sign language recognized:	Flemish Sign Language (2007), French Sign Language (2003)
Deaf sign language users:	4500 (Flanders) & 3000[6] (Wallonia)
Interpreters currently working:	160 (Flanders) & 12 (Wallonia)
Interpreter training program:	3 (Flanders: Mechelen, Gent, Antwerp)
Interpreter organization:	*Flanders*: Beroepsvereniging Vlaamse Gebarentaal Tolken (BVGT), www.bvgt.be
	Wallonia: Association Belge Francophone des Interprètes en Langue des Signes (ABILS) www.abils.net

Bosnia-Herzegovina

Population:	3,752,228
Area:	51,197 sq km
Spoken language:	Bosnian, Croatian, Serbian
Sign language:	Bosnian Sign Language
Sign language recognized:	2010
Deaf sign language Users:	20000
Interpreters currently working:	0
Interpreter training program:	0
Interpreter organization:	no

---

6. Survey 2004, response from ABILS

Croatia

Population:	4,407,00
Area:	56,542 sq km
Spoken language:	Croatian, Italian
Sign language:	Croatian Sign Language
Sign language recognized:	no
Deaf sign language Users:	1200[7] & 350 Deafblind sign language users
Interpreters currently working:	?
Interpreter training program:	0
Interpreter organization:	no

Cyprus

Population:	1,116,564
Area:	9,251 sq km
Spoken language:	Greek, Turkish
Sign language:	Cypriot Sign Language
Sign language recognized:	2006
Deaf sign language Users:	1000
Interpreters currently working:	15
Interpreter training program:	0
Interpreter organization: no	

Czech Republic

Population:	10,546,000
Area:	78,866 sq km
Spoken language:	Czech
Sign language:	Czech Sign Language
Sign language recognized:	1998
Deaf sign language Users:	10,000
Interpreters currently working:	60 - 80
Interpreter training program:	2
Interpreter organization:	Česká komora tlumočníků znakového jazyka
	e-mail: info@cktzj.com
	web site: www.cktzj.com/

Denmark

Population:	5,574,000
Area:	43,094 sq km
Spoken language:	Danish, Faroese, Greenlandic (an Inuit dialect), German (small minority)
Sign language:	Danish Sign Language
Sign language recognized:	no
Deaf sign language users:	4000 - 5000
Interpreters currently working:	300 - 350
Interpreter training program:	1
Interpreter organization:	Foreningen af Tegnsprogstolke (FTT)
	e-mail: info@tegnsprogstolk.dk
	web site: www.tegnsprogstolk.dk

---

7. Survey 2007, response from Croatia

England, Wales & Northern Ireland

Population:	57,039,900[8]
Area:	244,820 sq km (incl. Scotland)
Spoken language:	English, Welsh, Irish, Cornish
Sign language:	British Sign Language (BSL)
Sign language recognized:	2003
Deaf sign language users:	50,000
Interpreters currently working:	more than 700
Interpreter training program:	various (see chapter 2, education)
Interpreter organization:	Association of Sign Language Interpreters for England, Wales & Northern Ireland (ASLI)
	e-mail: info@asli.org.uk
	web site: www.asli.org.uk

Estonia

Population:	1,340,000
Area:	45,226 sq km
Spoken language:	Estonian
Sign language:	Estonian Sign Language
Sign language recognized:	2007
Deaf sign language users:	1500 - 2000
Interpreters currently working:	25
Interpreter training program:	1
Interpreter organization:	Eesti Viipekeele Tõlkide Ühing (EVTU)
	e-mail: evkty@evkty.ee
	web site: http://evkty.ee/joomla/

Finland

Population:	5,387,000
Area:	337,030 sq km
Spoken language:	Finnish, Swedish
Sign language:	Finnish Sign Language, Finnish-Swedish Sign Language
Sign language recognized:	1995[9]
Deaf sign language users:	5000
Interpreters currently working:	600 - 700
Interpreter training program:	2
Interpreter organization:	Suomen Viitomakielen Tulkit (SVT)
	e-mail: board@tulkit.net
	web site: www.tulkit.net

France

Population:	65,436,552
Area:	547,030 sq km
Spoken language:	French
Sign language:	French Sign Language
Sign language recognized:	2005
Deaf sign language users:	100,000
Interpreters currently working:	360
Interpreter training program:	5
Interpreter organization:	Association Francaise des Interprètes en Langue des Signes (AFILS)
	e-mail: contact@afils.fr, web site: www.afils.fr

---

8. http://www.ons.gov.uk/ons/rel/pop-estimate/population-estimates-for-uk--england-and-wales--scotland-and-northern-ireland/population-estimates-timeseries-1971-to-current-year/index.html (Last accessed 26 November 2012)

9. Sign Languages of Europe-Future Chances, Vera Krausneker, April 2000

Germany
Population: 81,726,000
Area: 357,021 sq km
Spoken language: German
Sign language: German Sign Language
Sign language recognized: 2002
Deaf sign language users: 200,000
Interpreters currently working: 600[10]
Interpreter training program: More than 5
Interpreter organization: Bundesverband der Gebardensprachdolmetscher innen Deutschlands e.V. (BGSD)
                                  e-mail: info@bgsd.de
                                  web site: www.bgsd.de

Greece
Population: 11,304,000
Area: 131,990 sq km
Spoken language: Greek
Sign language: Greek Sign Language
Sign language recognized: 2001
Deaf sign language Users: 5000
Interpreters currently working: 40
Interpreter training program: 0
Interpreter organization: SDENG
                                  e-mail: sdeng.gr@gmail.com

Hungary
Population: 9,971,000
Area: 93,030 sq km
Spoken language: Hungarian
Sign language: Hungarian Sign Language
Sign language recognized: 2009
Deaf sign language users: 9,000
Interpreters currently working: 70 - 90
Interpreter training program: 2
Interpreter organization: Jelnyelvi Tolmácsok Országos Szövetsége (JOSZ)
                                  e-mail: info@josz.hu
                                  website: www.josz.hu

Iceland
Population: 319,000
Area: 103,000 sq km
Spoken language: Icelandic
Sign language: Icelandic Sign Language
Sign language recognized: 2011
Deaf sign language users: 250
Interpreters currently working: 27
Interpreter training program: 1
Interpreter organization: HART
                                  e-mail: lkm@simnet.is

---

10. Survey 2007, response BGSD

Ireland

Population:	4,487,000
Area:	70,280 sq km
Spoken language:	Irish Gaeli, English
Sign language:	Irish Sign Language
Sign language recognized:	no
Deaf sign language users:	4500
Interpreters currently working:	60
Interpreter training program:	1
Interpreter organization:	Council of Sign Language Interpreters (CISLI)
	e-mail: cisli.ireland@gmail.com

Italy

Population:	57,634,327
Area:	301,230 sq km
Spoken language:	Italian (official), German (parts of Trentino-Alto Adige region are predominantly German speaking), French (small French-speaking minority in Valle d'Aosta region), Slovene (Slovene-speaking minority in the Trieste-Gorizia area)
Sign language:	Italian Sign Language
Sign language recognized:	no
Deaf sign language users:	40,000
Interpreters currently working:	200 (ANIMU) & 100 (ANIOS)
Interpreter training program:	0
Interpreter organization:	ANIOS: www.anios.it
	ANIMU: www.animu.it

Kosovo

Population:	1,794,303
Area:	10,908 sq km
Spoken language:	Albanian, Serbian
Sign language:	Kosovar Sign Language
Sign language recognized:	2010
Deaf sign language Users:	8000[11]
Interpreters currently working:	12
Interpreter training program:	1
Interpreter organization:	KASLI
	e-mail: kaslipresident@live.com

Latvia

Population:	2,220,000
Area:	64,589 sq km
Spoken language:	Latvian
Sign language:	Latvian Sign Language
Sign language recognized:	1999
Deaf sign language users:	2000
Interpreters currently working:	20
Interpreter training program:	1
Interpreter organization:	no

Lithuania

Population:	3,525,761
Area:	65,300 sq km
Spoken language:	Lithuanian
Sign language:	Lithuanian Sign Language

---

11. www.finlandkosovo.org/public/default.aspx?contentid=197139&nodeid=42593&contentlan=2&culture=en-US (Last accessed 12 December 2012)

Sign language recognized:	1995
Deaf sign language Users:	5000 - 8000
Interpreters currently working:	100
Interpreter training program:	1
Interpreter organization:	Lietuvos gestu kalbos verteju asociacija (LGKVA)
	e-mail: gkva.lt@gmail.com
	web site: www.lgkva.lt

Malta

Population:	419,000
Area:	316 sq km
Spoken language:	Maltese, English
Sign language:	Maltese Sign Language
Sign language recognized:	no
Deaf sign language users:	200
Interpreters currently working:	3 full time and 4 part time
Interpreter training program:	0
Interpreter organization:	no

Netherlands

Population:	16,696,000
Area:	41,532 sq km
Spoken language:	Dutch, Frisian
Sign language:	Dutch Sign Language
Sign language recognized:	no
Deaf sign language users:	7,5000
Interpreters currently working:	400
Interpreter training program:	1
Interpreter organization:	Nederlandse Beroepsvereniging Tolken Gebarentaal (NBTG)
	e-mail: info@nbtg.nl
	web site: www.nbtg.nl

Norway

Population:	4,952,000
Area:	324,220 sq km
Spoken language:	Norwegian
Sign language:	Norwegian Sign Language
Sign language recognized:	no
Deaf sign language users:	2500
Interpreters currently working:	500
Interpreter training program:	3
Interpreter organization:	Tolkeforbundet (Norwegian Association of Interpreters)
	e-mail: forbundsstyret@tolkeforbundet.no
	web site: www.tolkeforbundet.no

Poland

Population:	38,216,00
Area:	312,685 sq km
Spoken language:	Polish
Sign language:	Polish Sign Language
Sign language recognized:	2012
Deaf sign language users:	50,000
Interpreters currently working:	200
Interpreter training program:	1
Interpreter organization:	Stowarzyszenie Tłumaczy Polskiego Języka Migowego (STPJM)
	e-mail: biuro@stpjm.org.pl
	web site: www.stpjm.org.pl

Portugal

Population:	10,637,000
Area:	92,391 sq km
Spoken language:	Portuguese
Sign language:	Portugese Sign Language
Sign language recognized:	1997[12]
Deaf sign language users:	60000[13]
Interpreters currently working:	100
Interpreter training program:	4
Interpreter organization:	Associação Nacional e Profissional da Interpretação - Língua Gestual
	e-mail: anapilg.dir@gmail.com

Romania

Population:	21,390,000
Area:	237,500 sq km
Spoken language:	Romanian
Sign language:	Romanian Sign Language
Sign language recognized:	1999
Deaf sign language users:	24601
Interpreters currently working:	33
Interpreter training program:	2
Interpreter organization:	Asociaţia Naţională a Interpreţilor în Limbaj Mimico-Gestual (ANILMG)
	e-mail: anialmg_rom@yahoo.com
	web site: www.ailg.ro

Russia

Population:	141,930,000
Area:	
Spoken language:	Russian
Sign language:	Russian Sign Language
Sign language recognized:	no
Deaf sign language Users:	140,000
Interpreters currently working:	820
Interpreter training program:	5 or more
Interpreter organization:	региональная общественная организация "Объединения переводчиков жестового языка"
	e-mail: roo-opgy@mail.ru
	web site: www.rasli.ru

Scotland

Population:	5,254,800
Area:	78,782 sq km
Spoken language:	Scots, English, Gaelic
Sign language:	British Sign Language
Sign language recognized:	2011
Deaf sign language users:	7,000
Interpreters currently working:	80
Interpreter training program:	1
Interpreter organization:	Scottish Association of Sign Language Interpreters (SASLI)
	e-mail: mail@sasli.org.uk
	web site: www.sasli.org.uk

---

12. Sign Languages of Europe-Future Chances, Vera Krausneker, April 2000

13. Survey 2007, reply from Portugal

Serbia

Population:	7,261,000
Area:	88,361 sq km
Spoken language:	Serbian
Sign language:	Serbian Sign Language
Sign language recognized:	no
Deaf sign language Users:	30,000
Interpreters currently working:	50
Interpreter training program:	1
Interpreter organizations:	Asocijacija tumača srpskog znakovnog jezika (ATSZJ)

> e-mail: asocijacijatumacaszj@gmail.com
> web site: www.atszj.org
Udruzenje tumaca za lica ostecenoh sluha Srbije (UTLOSS)
> e-mail: utloss@gmail.com
> web site: www.utloss.rs

Slovenia

Population:	2,052,000
Area:	20,273 sq km
Spoken language:	Slovene
Sign language:	Slovenian Sign Language
Sign language recognized:	2002
Deaf sign language Users:	863
Interpreters currently working:	44
Interpreter training program:	1
Interpreter organization:	Zavod Združenje tolmačev za slovenski znakovni jezik (ZTZSJ)

e-mail: zdruzenjet@t-2.net
web site: www.tolmaci.si

Spain

Population:	47,190,493
Area:	505,992 sq km
Spoken language:	Spanish, Basque, Catalan, Galician, Occitan
Sign language:	Catalan Sign Language, Spanish Sign Language, Valencian Sign Language
Sign language recognized:	2007
Deaf sign language Users:	100,000 (no clear figures)
Interpreters currently working:	667
Interpreter training program:	4
Interpreter organization:	Federación Española de Intérpretes de Lengua de Signos y Guía-Intérpretes (FILSE)

e-mail: filse@filse.org
web site: www.filse.org

Sweden

Population:	9,453,000
Area:	449,964 sq km
Spoken language:	Swedish
Sign language:	Swedish Sign Language
Sign language recognized:	1981
Deaf sign language users:	10,000[14]
Interpreters currently working:	600[15]
Interpreter training program:	5 or more

---

14. Survey 2007, STTF response

15. Survey 2007, STTF response

Interpreter organization:	Sveriges teckenspråkstolkars förenings (STTF)
	e-mail: sttf@sttf.nu
	web site: www.sttf.nu

Switzerland

Population:	7,907,000
Area:	41,290 sq km
Spoken language:	German (63.7%), French (20.4%), Italian (6.5%), Roman (0.5%)

German speaking part

Sign language:	German Sign Language
Sign language recognized:	no
Deaf sign language users:	5000
Interpreters currently working:	52
Interpreter training program:	1
Interpreter organization:	Berufsvereinigung des Gebärdensprache Dolmetschers (BGD)
	e-mail: bgd@vpod-zh.ch
	Web site: www.bgd.ch

French speaking part

Sign language:	French Sign Language
Sign language recognized:	2010
Deaf sign language users:	2000
Interpreters currently working:	30
Interpreter training program:	0
Interpreter organization:	Association Romande de Interpretes en Langue des Signes (ARILS)
	e-mail: comite.arils@gmail.com

Italian speaking part

Sign language:	Italian Sign Language
Sign language recognized:	no
Deaf sign language users:	30
Interpreters currently working:	7
Interpreter training program:	0
Interpreter organization:	Interpreti Lingua Italiana dei Segni della Svittera Italiano (ILISSI)
	e-mail: ilissi@bluemail.ch

Ukraine

Population:	45,706.100
Area:	603,628 sq km
Spoken language:	Ukrainian
Sign language:	Ukrainian Sign Language
Sign language recognized:	2011
Deaf sign language Users:	150,000
Interpreters currently working:	350
Interpreter training program:	2
Interpreter organization:	no

APPENDIX 7 – OVERVIEW OF ALL GRAPHS

Part 1

1.1   Year of establishment of independent interpreter organizations
1.2   Sign Language Interpreters and national organizations: relative membership
1.3   Number of interpreters that are a member of their national or regional organization
1.4   Number of interpreters & non-interpreter members who are a member of the national or regional organization
1.5   Number of Sign Language Interpreters in 23 European countries, estimated by membership percentage of the corresponding national assocation
1.6   National organizations - individual interpreter membership fee (in Euros)
1.7   Total individual membership fees per year per national association (in Euros)
1.8   Number of registered interpreters in those countries & regions with a registry

Part 2

2.1   Number of interpreter educational programs
2.2   Overview of sign language interpreting programs in Europe
2.3   Number of educational programs in Europe per educational level
2.4   Number of students currently enrolled an interpreter training program
2.5   Total number of students who graduated from an interpreter training program

Part 3

3.1   Currently working sign language interpreters
3.2   Number of working interpreters compared: 2001, 2004, 2007, 2012
3.3   Deaf sign language users
3.4   Deaf sign language users per interpreter
3.5   Sign language recognition per country or region
3.6   Percentage of countries – forms of employment
3.7a   Employment forms per country and region
3.7b   Other employment forms per country and region
3.8   Employment setting: responsible party for the payment of interpreting services
3.9   Educational setting: responsible party for the payment of interpreting services
3.10   Medical setting: responsible party for the payment of interpreting services
3.11   Legal setting: responsible party for the payment of interpreting services
3.12   Theatre setting: responsible party for the payment of interpreting services
3.13   Interpreting services funded by
3.14   Range of minimum fees in euros per hour country/region
3.15   Minimum interpreting fee in euro per freelance hour
3.16   Overview per country of payment for freelance interpreting

REFERENCES

Calle, L. (2011). *The Right to Sign Language Interpreting Services when Working or Studying Abroad.* efsli report 2011

Calle, L. (2012a). *Sign Language Interpreter Training Programmes.* efsli report 2011, updated 2012

Calle, L. (2012b). *New Skills and Professional Profiles Required for the Sign Language Interpreter Profession in Europe.* efsli report 2012

Herreweghe, M. van & M. van Nuffel (2000). 'Sign (Language) Interpreting in Flanders, Belgium'. *RID Journal of Interpretation*, 101 - 130

Kalata-Zawlocka, A. (2012). 'The First Conference of the Association of Polish Sign Language Interpreters'. *efsli Newsletter*, Spring 2012, 7

Krausneker, V. (2000). *Sign Languages of Europe – Future chances,* paper presented at the EUD Celebratory Conference, Gent, Belgium, April 2000.

Krausneker, V. (2008). *The protection and promotion of sign languages and the rights of their users in Council of Europe member states: needs analysis.* Strasbourg: Council of Europe.

Misko, J. (2011). How do we perceive ourselves as interpreters and how do'those we serve perceive us?'. *efsli Newsletter*, March 2011, 7

Wheatley, M. & A. Pabsch (2012). *Sign Language Legislation in the European Union, Edition II.* Brussels: EUD.

Wit, M. de & M. Wheatley (forthcoming) . 'Joint Cooperation: The Only Way Forward'. *WASLI conference proceedings 2011.*

Wit, de M. (2008). *Sign Language Interpreting in Europe*, 2008 edition. Baarn: M. de Wit

Žižić, D. (2011). 'ATSZJ'. *efsli Newsletter*, March 2011, 8

Reports

Instruments for Lifting Language Barriers in Intercultural Legal Proceedings (2005). EU project JAI/2003/AGIS/048, ITV Hogeschool voor Tolken en Vertalen, Utrecht.

Report *Meer dan een Gebaar* (1997). Report of the Commission on the recognition of Dutch Sign Language.

Internet

Ethnologue Language Database: www.ethnologue.com

INDEX

Printed in Great Britain
by Amazon.co.uk, Ltd.,
Marston Gate.